PRESENTATIONS FOR DECISION MAKERS

Strategies for Structuring and Delivering Your Ideas

Marya W. Holcombe and Judith K. Stein

VNR VAN NOSTRAND REINHOLD COMPANY
—————————— *New York*

Copyright © 1983 by Van Nostrand Reinhold
Library of Congress Catalog Card Number 83-11322
ISBN 0-534-02704-0

Printed in the United States of America

Designed by Bill Agee

Van Nostrand Reinhold Company Inc.
115 Fifth Avenue
New York, New York 10003

Van Nostrand Reinhold Company Limited
Molly Millars Lane
Wokingham, Berkshire RG11 2PY, England

Van Nostrand Reinhold
480 La Trobe Street
Melbourne, Victoria 3000, Australia

Macmillan of Canada
Division of Canada Publishing Corporation
164 Commander Boulevard
Agincourt, Ontario M1S 3C7, Canada

16 15 14 13 12 11 10 9 8 7 6 5 4

Library of Congress Cataloging-in-Publication Data

Holcombe, Marya W.
      Presentations for decision makers.

      1. Communication in management.   2. Meetings.
I. Stein, Judith K.   II. Title.
HD30.3.H63   1983   658.4′5   83-11322
ISBN 0-534-02704-0

CONTENTS

What This Book Is About

Presentations for Decision Makers is designed to help you, as a manager, develop and deliver the oral presentations that are part of your job. Effective management depends on communication—both written and oral—and although many people feel their writing skills are adequate, almost no one confronts the task of giving an oral presentation without some qualms.

This book offers you a pragmatic and structured system for preparing a presentation as well as advice on how to deliver it with confidence and handle questions without discomfort. Specifically, by building on skills you already have, the techniques in this book equip you to:
- Decide on a strategy for success
- Analyze your audience
- Develop a logical and persuasive argument
- Transform your argument into a compelling presentation
- Design, make, and use visual aids
- Give the presentation
- Manage the question-and-answer session
- Apply these skills to meetings, negotiations, and videoconferences

Although any management communication that requires forethought and preparation, whether it is written or oral, can be defined as a presentation, in this book, we use the term *presentation* to mean an oral presentation unless we state otherwise. And, because for most managers the stakes are highest in a formal, internal presentation, we use this form as the focus of discussion, expanding on the applicability of the techniques to other situations.

Throughout the book, our purpose is to give a system that will be useful in a wide range of management settings. The material in the early chapters deals primarily with focus and structure, and should be useful in solving problems and writing as well as in designing and giving presentations and participating in meetings and informal exchanges. Much of the information in later chapters deals with how you present yourself and applies equally well whether you are speaking with one person or many. We also provide guidelines and checklists to help you anticipate crises and insure that you are well prepared. We suggest you read through the book once, and then follow the advice in it step by step as you develop your next presentation.

Armed with logical argument, well-designed visuals, and the confidence that comes from preparation and rehearsal, you will be able to walk into any conference room or auditorium ready to do your best.

MWH
JKS

Acknowledgments

This book owes its genesis to presenters, past and present. It is, after all, a distillation of all the things they've taught us as we've worked with them, listened to them, and given them suggestions. A successful presentation is one that "works," and we owe much of our practical knowledge to those who tried new styles and structures and let us participate in the process.

Many people helped us immeasurably by reading early drafts of chapters. We are especially grateful to Mark Bassin, Craig Bossi, Rick Hunt, Tom Strong and Gene Zelazny for their advice and encouragement. We owe special thanks, also, to those videoconference "veterans" who shared their experiences with us—Dick Jackson, Ira Katz, Phil Lichtenfels and Alan Ramsey. Phil Dorn, as always, helped us get the "categories" right. Our colleagues in the Management Communication Association and the ABCA shared ideas and argued the merits of our concepts— this book is far richer for their contributions.

Two people stand out for their quiet support as well as for their yeoman-like efforts: Marianne Ficocelli, our secretary, whose good humor through countless revisions (we are grateful she stopped counting) kept our spirits up and the pages moving, and Steve Keeble, our editor, who managed a process that spanned the continent.

In writing this book, husbands and children have often come last—we thank you.

1

A STRATEGY FOR SUCCESSFUL PRESENTATIONS

To insure success, any manager developing a presentation should first:
- Think about what makes a management presentation unique
- Develop a strategy that includes
  —Building consensus
  —Selecting the appropriate method
  —Writing an objective

Because a management presentation always seeks to promote action by an audience that has a stake in the outcome of the presentation, preparation requires strategic as well as tactical thinking. The first step is to understand how the nature of a management presentation influences your choice of strategies.

The Nature of Management Presentations

Management presentations are made to internal audiences (superiors, peers, or subordinates) and to external audiences (stockholders, customers, the press). The presenter should gear the message to the audience. An audience of superiors, peers, or customers will usually be asked to *make* a decision now or in the future. Even a presentation in which only preliminary findings are offered, a report on a research project, for example, is intended to stimulate action—usually approval for the next steps. Subordinates, stockholders, and even the press are more likely to be asked to *accept* a decision. Presenters sometimes forget that even though such a presentation ostensibly conveys orders or explains a situation—a new policy or a decline in earnings, perhaps—no audience acquiesces passively. Just as managers must convince their subordinates that a course of action makes sense before they can hope for enthusiastic implementation, the CEO must convince stockholders that declining earnings are not attributable to inept management if he or she wants to avoid conflict.

Because in a management presentation your audience has a stake in what you say, you can assume that the basic interest level is far higher than that of an audience listening idly to an after-dinner speech. As a result, the level of participation associated with a presentation is markedly higher than that associated with a formal speech, in which questions, if allowed at all, are entertained at the end (when the audience has generally forgotten the issues and simply wants to go home). In a management presentation you encourage participation, knowing that people who contribute are more likely to make a commitment to the action you propose.

Knowing that you want action and that people who are affected by a decision are more likely to agree to it if they have had a part in it, you can begin to create a successful presentation strategy.

Develop a Strategy

The management presentation process begins with the person (you or someone else) who has perceived a problem or opportunity. Because change involves risk, some organizations, like some people, find themselves frozen into senseless patterns as a result of inertia and fear of the unknown. Other organizations seem to be committed to change for change's sake. Like an executive who accepts every transfer to avoid ever having to adjust to people and situations on a long-term basis, these organizations are constantly tinkering with systems, concepts, or policies in an effort to distract themselves from the responsibility of looking at the broader picture. Whether you've decided to recommend action or whether someone else has assigned you the task, you need to consider the organizational context and ask two searching questions:

Will action in this area be beneficial? The Oath of Hippocrates states: "If you can do no good, at least do no harm." Presenters, like doctors, should follow this advice. If something works well, leave it alone. Changing things requires time and effort. Don't squander your resources by altering something that's still working well.

Is this part of the system easily changed? If a real problem exists, can anything be done about it? Sometimes there is simply nothing you can do to improve the situation. If the U.S. Government, for example, is drowning your small business in paperwork, it's better to devise ways to cope than to fight a losing battle.

If you've found a target for change and you think you can make an impact, then you're ready to start down the long road that culminates in a presentation. Because no presentation can be successful without the support of others, you'll need to build consensus at each stage of the process.

Building Consensus

When you first become aware of a situation begging for change, you'll want to start the consensus-building process by talking with as many others as possible to enlist their support. You may find, of course, that others don't see it your way, and you'll then either drop the idea or wait for a more advantageous time. If you find that people are sympathetic to considering the need for change, you can hold some informal brainstorming sessions to generate ideas for dealing with the situation.

After you've explored the problem thoroughly, and after you've gathered together a group with sufficient clout to have a chance of prevailing, do the analytic problem solving necessary to arrive at a sound proposal. Once again, test the merits of the proposal with your supporters, and cycle back to an earlier point if you meet resistance. Finally, give serious thought to whether you or someone else should give the presentation itself.

Bridge-building of this sort is essential to the success of a presentation. New managers who lack confidence, and managers who have a strong ego involvement in a particular proposal, may ignore the necessity to build consensus, either because they fear someone will take credit for their ideas or because they suspect someone will sabotage the presentation if the ideas are revealed prematurely. Although these disasters do sometimes happen, failure to go through the "political" process of establishing a receptive audience virtually guarantees the presentation will be greeted with hostility or indifference. In general, the more you give (in terms of sharing ideas, strategies, problem-solving techniques) the more you get (in terms of other ideas, reality testing, and support).

As your proposal evolves from vague idea to detailed solution, your method for communicating with the members of the coalition you have developed and the decision makers you will be addressing becomes more and more formal. At each stage, though, you must choose the best communication method out of the several possibilities available to you.

Selecting the Appropriate Method

Your choice of method depends in part on your own skills as a presenter or writer and in part on your assessment of the peculiar demands and characteristics of your audience, which we discuss in chapter 2. In broad terms, choose an informal approach in the early stages of the process and a more formal approach in the later stages when firm decisions must be made. At any stage, you will have to decide whether a written, an oral, or a combined approach is best suited to the situation. Exhibit 1.1 provides a menu of possibilities.

Scribbled notes, huddles, and phone calls. In the early stages of decision making and for decisions that involve relatively few people, scribbled notes, huddles, and phone calls are fine. For the most part, these informal communications, because they involve people who know each other well, require little preparation. Participants may stop one another in the hall, for example, or write notes back and forth. The decision element is generally confined to agreement that the writer or caller is on the right track in trying to solve the problem. There is very little potential for misunder-

Exhibit 1.1

SELECT THE APPROPRIATE COMMUNICATION METHOD

	Communication Method	Complexity and Sensitivity of Subject	Potential Degree of Misunderstanding	Record	Preparation Time
Oral (Informal)	Huddle	Relatively simple or sensitive	Little chance	None	Very little
	Phone call	Relatively simple or sensitive	Some chance (no access to facial or body cues)	Notes or memos	Little
Oral (Formal)	Meeting	Complex and/or wide-ranging	Little chance	Minutes or tapes	Preparation varies with complexity of subject; requires coordination and leadership
	Presentation	Complex; requires visual support	Little chance if questions encouraged	Handouts possible	Moderate to extensive; varies with complexity of subject and sophistication of supporting material
	Videoconference	Variably complex; may not be appropriate if security is an issue	Some chance (depends on capacity of system and leader to permit participants' interaction)	Notes or videotapes	Comparable to time required for meeting or presentation
Written (Informal)	Scribbled note	Simple; not sensitive	Some chance (notes are unedited)	Note itself; however, such notes frequently misplaced or destroyed	Little
	Electronic mail	Relatively simple and not sensitive	Great chance (writers are often careless)	System-generated hard copy or computer storage	Little
Written (Formal)	Memo or report	Simple, technical, or complex	Some chance if material is complex or writer is careless	Formal copies	Moderate to extensive; varies with complexity of subject

standing in either a huddle or a phone call, if people are acute observers of nonverbal cues. However, scribbled notes can be easily misinterpreted as curt or even abusive. It's easy to scrawl "What does this mean?" across a memo and return it to the sender, for example, but this kind of insensitivity, given the permanence of writing, is guaranteed to cause hurt feelings. Calling the person into your office and gently asking the same question is a safer procedure.

Electronic mail (EM). Another informal method used increasingly in the early stages of decision making is electronic mail (EM). Although these unedited messages go back and forth with a plethora of spelling and grammatical errors, the medium does encourage the quick response needed in the early stages of consensus building. Because this hybrid system provides a written substitute for conversation and still lacks conventions, it often leads to misunderstanding. Nevertheless, when time is short, this informal way of gathering information can be very functional for reaching a great many people quickly.

Meetings and memoranda. These moderately formal methods are helpful midway through the decision-making process. Although a meeting (defined here as an organized discussion) is primarily used for problem solving, it can also be used for approving specific actions that will eventually lead to a final solution. You can use a short memo in the same way. However, because people can ask and answer questions more easily in a meeting than through an exchange of memos, fewer misunderstandings result from meetings. Memos, on the other hand, can deal with more complex concepts—the structuring of an international financial deal, for example, or the detailed analysis of a new management information system. When you have complex material or you need an intermediate decision, choose a meeting or a memo over a phone call, huddle, note, or EM message.

Reports, oral presentations, and videoconferences. The long process of making an important proposal culminates in a formal report, a formal oral presentation, or both. Although by the time you get to this stage you know what you want to say, it still takes a substantial investment of time to craft a formal presentation, whether written or oral. These communications, which usually include the use of visuals, are expected to be professional in form as well as in content. In some organizations, when a recommendation involves the approval of decision makers in several locations, a videoconference is the selected approach. (How to choose among the various forms of videoconferences is discussed in chapter 10.)

At each stage of the process, then, you have the choice of speaking or writing. Because so much depends on the acceptance of others, and because reading something has a different emotional impact than hearing it, the choice is crucial—far more so than many managers believe.

Choosing Between an Oral and a Written Presentation

Once in a while, an inexperienced manager, asked to give an oral presentation, will write a report and read it to the audience. If you've ever squirmed through the embarrassment of attending such a "presentation," we don't have to tell you that there's a vast difference between oral and written presentations, and that what works in one form doesn't work in the other. Understanding the subtleties of the difference will help you choose the correct method at the outset.

The oral presentation. Oral presentations are generally more persuasive than written presentations, especially when combined with visual aids. Researchers who have tested the way the brain responds to such stimuli as language, visual images, and music have found that the spoken word engages both the right (creative, intuitive) and left (analytical, logical) sides of the brain, whereas the written word appeals more specifically to the left side. Since most managers seem to make decisions based on both rational and intuitive criteria, you are more likely to gain acceptance for your proposal through an oral presentation, which appeals to both sides, than through a report, which appeals to only one.

In addition, an oral presentation gives you more possibilities for building a relationship with your audience than does a memo or report. Spoken language has an immediate, magical quality that written language usually lacks. Rarely can the enthusiasm communicated in a phone call or a meeting be duplicated in a letter or memo. Although writers can reflect on their choice of words and use a far larger vocabulary than speakers, speakers can use inflection to give their ideas emphasis. One presenter says she can "feel" her energy motivate her audience—something difficult to imagine in the case of a writer. Similarly, although the recipient of a phone call cannot "see" gestures and facial expressions, he or she can "hear" the smile in a caller's voice. (Many phone solicitation companies train their employees to smile when they speak on the phone for precisely this reason.) It is simply true that most people come through better in person than in writing.

When your communication is intended to stimulate direct action, you must be able to evaluate the depth of the audience's understanding and degree of acceptance as you go along. While this checking is relatively easy when you are talking with someone in person or electronically, it is not possible in written communications in which the response is delayed and perhaps edited before it gets back to you. You have a better chance of knowing whether you are getting close to your ultimate goal when you see your audience's reactions than when you have to wait for written response.

It is also obvious that, as speaker, you can get valuable feedback during the presentation itself. As writer, you are far more limited. If a statement in a report or memo raises a question in the reader's mind that is not answered immediately, the reader may never understand the main point. If a member of the audience seems confused, however, a speaker can clarify a point either in the course of the presentation or during the question-and-answer period. If a writer misjudges the reader's need for information and produces a long-winded report, the writer has no control over the reader, who can simply ignore the report or throw it away. In contrast, a speaker can adjust to the audience. If listeners are restless, for example, you can adjust the timing; if they are bored, you can eliminate material. If they do not understand, you can give more information.

When dealing with a controversial subject, it is usually better to bring participants together in one room to discuss the matter rather than to circulate a written report or memo. When there's serious disagreement, the kinds of pencilled-in comments that tend to fuel conflict may accumulate as the memo ricochets from one desk to another. Confronting issues directly, and in person, is generally preferable to circulating paper—even though your writing skills may be keener than your ability to deal with opposition in person.

In the last analysis, however, no matter how strong your desire to make a presentation, you need to consider the feasibility of getting people together. Sometimes deadlines, the number of people involved, and access to equipment, either internal or through an outside contractor, make an oral presentation impossible. If a meeting cannot be arranged without seriously inconveniencing people, consider a written approach. In addition, there are often good reasons for preferring a memo or report.

The written memo or report. If participation is not necessary, a written document is far more economical than a full-scale oral presentation. Delivering the same message to a number of people orally takes a great deal more time than distributing copies of a memo or report. Furthermore, you can provoke antagonism if you ask people to interrupt their work for a meeting or presentation when the need is not readily apparent.

In addition, highly technical material is generally better handled in a written report than in an oral presentation. Sometimes an oral presentation on a technical topic works if the audience is composed of technicians, but, even then, the need to visualize complex relationships may dictate the use of diagrams, charts, or graphs of much finer quality than that possible in a visual presentation. Although handouts can be used to provide backup to an oral presentation, any material that requires careful analysis should be part of a written report.

If you're concerned about being quoted out of context, or if pre-

---

Guidelines for Selecting an Oral or Written Presentation

Select an oral presentation if you answer yes to these questions:
- Is the topic controversial?
- Do the people involved need to ask questions to understand the material?
- Is immediate action necessary?
- Can participants get together easily?

Select a written presentation if you answer yes to these questions:
- Does the audience need time to understand and absorb the material?
- Is a permanent record necessary to guard against misinterpretation?
- Is a discussion unimportant at this stage?

cise language is necessary to explain a technical topic, or if some kind of record is required, better write than speak.

The choice, then, between speaking or writing should depend on the need for participation or immediate agreement, the complexity of the material, the potential for conflict, and the need for a permanent record.

If you decide on an oral presentation, your first step is to write a clear objective.

Write a Specific Objective

Although all speakers should formulate objectives, management presenters have special obligations because, as we have emphasized, their presentations always anticipate an action. Logic is the key to persuasion for most managers. To insure that your argument makes logical sense to the audience for whom it is intended, as well as to set guidelines for research, and to establish standards for measuring your success, you must begin with an objective.

Focusing your presentation. If your presentation is intended to convince people to accept a decision you have already made, you can write a specific objective immediately. If you have been asked to solve a problem, your initial objective will be vague. For example, one objective might be to recommend a method for improving your company's inventory control. This rough objective helps give you a focus for solving the problem. Later, you can reword the objective to identify both the specific recommendation and the decision maker. For example, you might write: "Convince the Vice-President for Production to spend $20,000 to purchase the Century Data Inventory Control System." You cannot solve the problem without a rough objective, and you cannot develop the presentation without a specific one.

Limiting your audience. Because objectives identify the people who need to take action, they help you narrow the list of people you invite to the presentation (assuming you have control over this list). Only those people who will participate in the decision or need the information to do their jobs should attend. People with no vested interest in the discussion can be disruptive; winnowing them out is clearly beneficial.

Saving research time. Taking the time to formulate an objective may frustrate your desire to get started. However, by defining your objective, you save yourself from wading through every file remotely related to an issue in order to get a feel for the topic, or from undertaking extensive research that is ultimately unusable (or worse, used merely because so much time has been invested in it). Intelligent research is vital, but unguided meandering wastes time.

Measuring results. Finally, by clarifying your objective you will be able to judge the effectiveness of your presentation. You can't know whether you've succeeded unless you know what you intended. Since the objective includes the action you seek, success is easy to measure.

Examples of Objectives

To write a useful objective, ask yourself: What action do I want my audience to take as a result of this presentation? The response you create in your mind should be specific. The next question is: Who is the right person to take action? You should be able to visualize how the person or persons involved will take the action. In writing your objective, always try to isolate the decision maker or decision makers from others who may be present. Look at these examples.

Presenter	Vague Objective	Effective Objective
A staff member in a small venture-capital firm	Invest in Office Bank	Persuade the partners to invest $200,000 to fund the Office Bank, an innovative office-equipment supply house
The manager of the human resources department of a large industrial company	Give contract to the Self-Assessment Institute	Convince the Vice-President of Personnel to give the Self-Assessment Institute a contract to run a workshop in career planning for the managerial development program
A labor negotiator for a manufacturing firm	Freeze pay increases	Convince union representatives to accept a freeze on cost-of-living increases

Notice that the difference between a vague objective and an effective objective is the degree to which each specifies the outcome and identifies the person who will implement the proposal.

The objective may be more difficult to formulate if the audience is being asked to accept a decision. If you cannot write down what you want to achieve, however, it is unlikely that you will get the message across. Look at these examples.

Presenter	Vague Objective	Effective Objective
The head of a department who has just purchased a new word processing system	Explain how the new system will work	Convince members of the department to use the new system by explaining its value and showing them how it works
A bank branch manager who has just instituted a new retirement policy	Explain the new policy	Convince the employees that the new policy provides valuable new benefits
The head of a task force trying to determine the feasibility of "quality circles"	Provide a progress report	Persuade top management that work to date has been useful and we're on the right track

Although these presentations ostensibly explain or inform the audience, the effective objectives identify specific actions and the people who must take these actions, thereby providing more useful focus for the presentations.

Occasionally, you may have trouble identifying the decision maker for a specific presentation. For example, you have been asked to present a plan for a new product to your co-workers on the division marketing staff. The ultimate decision maker for the proposal is corporate top management. The support of the other staff members, however, will be necessary if the proposal is to be successfully implemented, and some of them will influence top management's decision. For your purposes, all the members of the staff are decision makers. If you are asked, later, to make the presentation to top management, you'll have to review your remarks and probably design a new presentation to meet the needs of that group.

In writing an objective, keep in mind that the decision maker is the person or persons in the room who will take action. These decision makers are the ones who will make or break your presentation. You'll learn more about them in the next chapter.

SUMMARY

Management presentations always seek to promote action by an audience that has a stake in the outcome of the presentation.
- The success of a formal presentation depends on agreement
- Different kinds of written and oral presentations are most effective at different stages in the consensus-building process
- At each stage the choice between a written and an oral approach depends on
  —the level of controversy
  —the complexity of the material
  —the need for immediate action
  —the need for a written report
- Writing a specific objective is a necessary step in developing any presentation because it helps to
  —focus the presentation
  —limit the audience
  —save research and problem-solving time
  —measure the effectiveness of the presentation
- An objective should state the action desired and identify the person who must be persuaded to act

2

FOCUSING ON THE AUDIENCE

Now that you have crafted a strategy and developed your objective, it is time to focus on your audience. For your presentation to have the best chance of success, you must know how to

- Select the participants
- Analyze the audience
- Choose the presenter

When you wrote the objective, you tentatively identified the decision maker—the person or persons who will take action on the basis of your presentation. Before you go on, you must decide who else should attend.

Selecting the Participants

Because any presentation should include discussion, you should invite only those people who will meaningfully contribute to the discussion and those who must accept the decision if it is to be implemented successfully. For decision making, it is advisable to limit the group to under eight people. The larger the group, the more difficult it is to keep the discussion focused on the problem. The size of the group is less crucial when your main purpose is to get the audience to support a decision already made. Although discussion in this case is beneficial, it is not critical. If you find that more people need to hear a presentation than your facilities can comfortably accommodate, consider giving several smaller presentations. People will feel flattered if the group is kept to a manageable size, and you'll have a better chance to win them over.

If you are making the presentation, you will generally draw up the list of attendees, or at least make suggestions about the group's composition. Although you may change the list as you work through the preparation process, you need some idea of who should attend to create a profile of your potential audience.

Analyzing the Audience

For most internal presentations, you'll know the members of your audience. Occasionally, if you're giving a command performance, you'll be talking to some people you've never met. Make sure you're informed in advance of everyone who may be coming to the presentation and do a little preliminary checking. Nothing is more unnerving than a walk-in appearance by the executive vice-president when you had planned an informal session with a few colleagues and subordinates.

Once you know who the members of your audience are, start to construct a picture of them, either by asking yourself a few pertinent questions about them (if you know most of them and the subject is relatively simple) or by filling out an audience profile, such as the one shown on page 17 (if the audience includes many people you don't know and the subject is relatively complex).

Filling out such a profile form forces you to take the needs of your audience into account when you're developing your presentation. It may also alert you to a recycling point. That is, as you think about your audience and its attitudes, you may realize that your preliminary attempts to build consensus have been inadequate. If you discover that members of your projected audience

---

AUDIENCE PROFILE

My objective in making this presentation (underline action):

Who is the decision maker or decision makers?

How much does the decision maker know about the situation?

How does the decision maker view the situation?

How will the decision maker react to the proposal?

What is the decision maker's style?

Who else will attend the presentation?
What are their views of the proposal?

Who else will be affected by this presentation?

What's the next step?

What is my revised objective or fallback position?

seriously disagree on the need for change, or are locked in apparently irreconcilable conflict, you may decide to defer your presentation until you have a better chance for success.

Write the objective at the very top of your audience profile and underline the action you hope to initiate if you have solved the problem. If you have not yet solved the problem, you will write a tentative objective and answer the questions as well as you can, knowing that you will revise the profile when you have a specific proposal in mind.

Who is the decision maker? Your objective should have identified the decision maker or decision makers. Even though you must take into account the needs of others in the audience, your presentation should be directed primarily toward the decision makers. If you're preparing a presentation for someone else to give, you may have difficulty determining who the true decision maker is. For example, if your boss asks you to develop a presentation to senior management, senior management is the decision maker for the presentation, but the initial decision maker is your boss. Try to nail down the focus by considering your boss as the decision maker who must first accept the presentation. If there are real conflicts between what she wants to happen and what you see as advisable, start negotiations quickly and reach some sort of agreement early in the game.

How much does the decision maker know about the situation? It's your obligation to narrow the scope of the presentation to include just the information the decision maker needs to have to understand your argument, no more. Any presentation, from the audience's point of view, is, in a sense, an imposition. Everyone feels he or she has left an important project in order to be present and, consequently, will view unnecessary detail with irritation. On the other hand, if members of the audience don't understand something and you don't go into enough detail, they have only two options: they can tune out and start mulling over a delicious fantasy, or they can interrupt you and ask for clarification. It's unlikely they'll interrupt, particularly if the audience includes people at different levels in the organization. The reasons for their reticence? They don't want to be considered uninformed ("I should have known that") or stupid ("I should be able to understand this").

In most cases, especially in internal presentations that represent the culmination of a long problem-solving process, the people involved already know a fair amount about both the problem and your approach to it. In the consensus-building stage, you talked to most of the decision makers, found out what they know, and kept them informed of your progress. Although you can't assume they will remember the details of these preliminaries, you can be sure they will remember the general drift.

The most difficult problems arise when you're dealing with something fairly technical or when the decision maker is new to the organization and doesn't know the history of the problem. In such cases, a preliminary briefing to bring the nontechnical people or the new decision maker up to speed is a necessity. You can't hope to educate listeners during the presentation—you don't have time.

How does the decision maker view the situation? One of the most common failings of presenters is to assume others view the problem the same way they do. A person's background influences his or her perceptions: A financial officer will look at a situation from a cost or earnings perspective; a marketing officer will look at the same set of data with a view to increasing market share; managers who have attended law school will look for legal ramifications. If you are to accumulate the most pertinent criteria for judging alternative proposals, you need to find out how the decision makers view the situation. You would not, for example, make a presentation to a financial vice-president that does not include a discussion of the costs involved in your proposal.

Once again, in most cases you already have some idea about what the decision maker thinks is the real problem, but if you have any question, ask. For example, if the executive vice-president says to you, "Please pull together some facts and propose some alternatives that the board can consider in dealing with the unfriendly takeover bid," don't jump to the conclusion that she's really saying, "Give me some strategies to buy time until we can find a white knight," just because that is what you want to hear.

On rare occasions, you won't be able to find out precisely how much the decision maker already knows, either about the genesis of the proposal or the particulars of the subject. In that case, you'll have to make some educated guesses based on what you know about the decision maker's background and education as well as his or her role in the organization. Considering someone's background does not mean indulging in stereotypes; it means thinking about how an individual will respond to a proposal based on his or her past experience, and gearing your presentation in terms of argument and language to maximize your chances of reaching that person. A case in point: The president of a small Midwestern firm, a self-made man who had never finished high school, was approached by a colleague who wanted him to support a museum in its quest to acquire some Remington bronzes. The colleague, wanting to demonstrate her cultural expertise, phrased the presentation in such arcane terms that the president, who had initially been interested in the subject, felt patronized and directed his support elsewhere. The colleague's mistake: failure to analyze her audience's background.

How will the decision maker react to the proposal? Predicting the decision maker's response isn't always easy. Not only are human beings unpredictable and sometimes eccentric, but each person may act quite differently as part of a group from the way he or she would respond individually. As a result, you may have a much easier time predicting how your boss will react to a presentation substantiating the need for more staff than predicting the reactions of the operating committee to the same plan. Not only do you lack day-to-day experience with each member of the larger group, but the relationships among its members may influence their behavior in the group and their reactions to your presentation.

Almost every presenter, at one time or another, has been forced to deal with hostile questions or interruptions from someone whose real goal was to show other participants his own expertise rather than to express honest disagreement. The better prepared you are for hostility, the better you will handle it. If you don't have a good grasp of the decision maker's view of the problem, your job is to find out. You have several ways of doing this:

- **Review the fate of similar proposals.** Do some digging. Were these proposals given a fair hearing or dismissed out of hand? Discover the fatal flaw in the last proposal and don't repeat it. Have conditions changed enough since the last round that you can reasonably make a case for a new hearing? By learning about the fate of other proposals, you can sense the organizational criteria used for previous decisions, especially if you're new on the job. For example, in some very large, older firms, the most important standard used to judge proposals is the degree of risk to which the company would be exposed if the proposal were adopted. Learning this (either through research or simply by asking questions) may be the most important discovery presenters in that firm ever make.

- **Consider whether your proposal will in some way reduce the power or influence of the decision maker.** When managers have a negative view of a proposal, it is frequently because they are concerned that it will threaten their own positions. If so, and if you can, be prepared to reassure them.
- **Recognize that there is a built-in bias in favor of status quo.** The burden of proof is on the one advocating change.
  Most often, the people you are presenting to have had something to do with the way things are now—asking them to change is asking them to admit they were wrong in the past. Because any advocate of change is at an immediate disadvantage, sweeping changes are less likely to gain acceptance than minor changes. If you sense opposition, you may want to start by proposing a minor but significant change and working up to a major systemic proposal.
- **Realize that if the decision maker is on record as opposing your proposal, it will be very difficult to gain acceptance.** People are reluctant to change course in public. Your work in the preliminary phases of the presentation process should be geared to averting any public stand by the people involved in taking action.

If, at any point along the way, you sense that there is strong opposition to your proposal, it's time to reassess the situation, considering whether a confrontation is worth it and perhaps delaying the presentation until a more propitious time.

What if you're giving a command performance or you can't control whether or not you give a presentation? Usually, you have more control than you think. Try negotiating with the person who gave you the assignment. Unless that person is bound by obligations to someone up the line or is deliberately sacrificing you in order to distract the audience from something else, he or she will usually be open to rescheduling the presentation or possibly shelving it completely. One thing for sure, you won't know whether this kind of readjustment is possible unless you ask. Giving a presentation is a great opportunity—don't waste it on lost causes.

Gauging possible reactions to a proposal can help you prevent some unpleasant surprises—but not all of them. One presenter, who had checked the major thrust of his presentation with his boss and received an enthusiastic endorsement, got caught in crossfire when another member of the audience attacked both his argument and his credentials on the way to proposing her own pet project as a more worthy alternative. Only later did the presenter and his boss find out that the president had given the same assignment to two people in an effort to get excellence through competition. However one views the president's managerial style, the presenter could not have anticipated the attack. The fate of his presentation, in reality, was out of his control.

What is the decision maker's style? By knowing how the decision maker deals with people, you can develop a presentation to fit his or her style. You should refer to this question again before you design the final presentation because the answer will help you anticipate difficulties. To counter an authoritarian decision maker who interrupts constantly, for example, be prepared to summarize repeatedly to bring the audience back to the point. You may even want to announce a time schedule in advance. Then you can use the schedule as an excuse for regaining control after one of the inevitable interruptions. Once you've lost control of the presentation, it is difficult to get it back. For example, at the end of one presentation, the chairman of the board turned to the rest of the group and, ignoring the presenter, asked: "Are there any *intelligent* questions?" Total silence ensued as the presenter stood by helplessly while members of the audience evaluated their questions and found them wanting. By taking control of the presentation early on, this kind of embarrassment might have been avoided. By asserting control, you can also deal with the decision maker who is so sold on participation that he or she never comes to the point. Without your control, a question session could dissolve into a welter of trivia and, as one fed-up manager put it, "long discussions on how we should be discussing the issue."

The decision maker's style also influences the presentation format you choose. Does the decision maker want "all the figures"? If so, use tables in your handouts instead of graphs or charts. Is he suspicious of "computer magic"? Don't haul in your personal computer to convince him that you've done your homework. Is she an informal person who's more inclined to pop into your office for a talk than to write you a memo? Put on a presentation that's professional but not slick. If you're dealing with two decision makers with different styles, try to adjust to both if you can comfortably do so. For example, use graphs or overhead transparencies for the one who responds to visual representations and provide a handout that includes all of the relevant figures for the other. Otherwise, concentrate on the most supportive decision maker. You will perform better and, therefore, increase the likelihood of persuading everyone in the audience.

Who else will attend the presentation? What are their views of the proposal? Since most of the people in the audience, aside from the decision maker, will influence the outcome of the presentation in some way, try to meet their needs as well. Usually this means involving them in discussions before and during the presentation to insure that they are satisfied with any implementation plan you're proposing. It also means being prepared to confront any hostile views. The more involvement you get from the participants the more likely you'll be to make an impact. Proposals usually wither because someone forgets to make sure that the people involved accept the change. The key is to ask them what they think rather than tell them what you think. If this group includes people you don't know, memorize their names or write them down in advance so you'll be able to call on them by name if they raise questions.

Who else will be affected by this presentation? There's a possibility of misinterpretation in any communication and that possibility becomes greater as the message is repeated. For most far-reaching decisions, many more people are affected by the decision than are present when the proposal is made. Usually word of impending change starts along the grapevine as soon as the presentation ends. Frequently a very human tendency to exaggerate takes over ("They said there were only two alternatives—to disband the chemical sales division or to lay off 10% of our sales force") and the result is a good deal of damage. Although you cannot eliminate all the problems involved in secondhand and thirdhand communication, using precise language will help. In addition, you can try to identify the people who need to know about the presentation and have someone who has credibility explain the outcome to them in person.

What's the next step? Constructing a persuasive argument for your course of action isn't enough. Managers are hired and retained for their ability to make decisions and take action. People are more comfortable if they know what they are expected to do next to get the action going. In fact, merely stating the next step may move them past debating the virtue of the proposal and on to a consideration of how they can do what you ask.

What's my fallback position? After you have analyzed the audience, go back to your objective. Is it realistic? Even if you haven't encountered enough opposition to consider additional support-building or a temporary delay, you may decide that your objective is too ambitious. If so, revise it. Also, consider a fallback position—an objective that would be acceptable if opposition to your original objective surfaces during the presentation. The staff member in the venture-capital firm who wanted the partners to invest $200,000 in a project, for example, might have felt comfortable with an investment of $150,000 as long as other conditions were met. Although you should generally be prepared to negotiate (nothing does less for a presenter than total rigidity and a refusal to entertain other possibilities), always ask for what you want. If you ask for less, that's what you'll get.

You need not spend too much time filling out the audience profile. The profile in Exhibit 2.1 was filled out by a manager who wanted her presentation to convince top management to buy an in-house EDP system. A few phrases were all that were necessary.

Choosing the Most Effective Presenter

As the person most concerned with initiating change (even though originally someone else may have given you the mandate), you are responsible for determining who will be the most effective presenter for the situation. By the time you finish this book, your skills should be on a par with those of anyone in your organization, but persuasion depends on intangibles as well. For example, how much credibility do you have with the audience? If you are a relative newcomer to the organization, even if you have done most of the groundwork, you may be better off suggesting that someone higher up give the presentation. The success of the proposal is far more important than any points you may win by presenting it—and the greater the status of the presenter, the more likely the proposal is to succeed. Generally speaking, proposals are submitted for approval at upper levels. Since people are persuaded by those who are similar to themselves, passing the baton to someone higher up may mean the difference between success and failure.

If you have an intense emotional involvement with the success of the proposal, you have even more reason to seek an alternate speaker. A more dispassionate speaker may well be more effective, since most managers (like many sophisticated audiences) tend to read a high level of emotion as lack of objectivity. If members of an audience feel the speaker is heavily invested in the outcome, they may question the validity of his or her argument. Remember, of course, that emotionalism is different from feeling and commit-

Exhibit 2.1

AUDIENCE PROFILE

My objective in making this presentation (underline action):

TO PERSUADE SENIOR MANAGEMENT TO INSTITUTE AN
IN-HOUSE EDP INVENTORY MANAGEMENT SYSTEM.

Who is the decision maker or decisions makers?

JOHN HUBERT   SAM JANES   DEBBIE WENTWORTH

How much does the decision maker know about the situation?

KNOW WE NEED BETTER INVENTORY CONTROL BUT DON'T
KNOW DETAILS ABOUT AVAILABLE ALTERNATIVES,

How does the decision maker view the situation?

CONCERNED PRIMARILY WITH SAVING MONEY.
SAM DOES NOT WANT TO FIRE ANYONE.

How will the decision maker react to the proposal?

OK— NOT COMMITTED TO ANY SPECIFIC PROPOSAL.

What is the decision maker's style?

JOHN WANTS ALL THE OPTIONS LAID OUT.

Who else will attend the presentation?
What are their view of the proposal?

PURCHASING AGENT — NO OPINION
SOMEONE FROM COMPTROLLER'S OFFICE — DON'T KNOW

Who else will be affected by this presentation?

NO ONE

What's the next step?

REQUEST FUNDS FOR NEXT QUARTER.

What is my revised objective or fallback position?

(NO FALLBACK)

ment—both of which are prerequisites if you are to persuade people to undertake any major change. If it's your choice, and you decide you are not the best person to present, choose a presenter carefully.

We've been talking about one presenter here, largely because we feel team presentations are usually an invitation to disaster. It's odd that team members, many of whom are quick to acknowledge individual differences of other sorts (perhaps one has especially creative ideas or another is a lucid writer), often decide to give everyone a piece of the action when it comes to making a presentation. We've seen reasonably successful two-person presentations, but the people involved had worked together for years and had thrashed out most of their problems concerning competition and competence. By and large, though, team presentations have distinct disadvantages. For one thing, the members of the audience may be confused because they cannot determine who's in charge. In addition, any lapse in the intricate coordination necessary to shift from one presenter to another may result in pathetic silences or comical babble. Worse yet, when things don't go well, the members of the team may turn on each other.

Guidelines for Selecting a Presenter

- How extensive is the person's knowledge of the topic?
- Can he or she be instructed fairly quickly?
- How much credibility does the person have with the audience?
- Can the person be objective about the proposal?
- Does the person have good presentation skills?

Once you have a clear understanding of your audience, you can begin to construct an argument that will lead to the action you want. Techniques for building such an argument are the subject of the next chapter.

SUMMARY

To design an effective presentation, you must satisfy the needs of your audience, a task that involves:
- Selecting the right participants
  —choose people who have a stake in the decision.
  —keep the group to a manageable size

- Analyzing the audience
  —find out the decision maker's level of knowledge, biases, view of the proposal, and style
  —consider who else will be attending
  —think about who else in the organization will be affected
- Choosing the most effective presenter
  —pick someone who is knowledgeable, credible, and skillful
  —avoid team presentations

3

BUILDING A LOGICAL STRUCTURE

To be effective, management presenters depend on logic. Whether your presentation proposes a recommendation or defends one alternative over another, you need a logical structure for your ideas. That structure is obtained by:

- Establishing concrete criteria
- Developing an organization tree
- Ordering your points effectively

Every presentation should have a beginning that draws the audience in and provides guidelines for the argument to follow; a body that makes the argument; and an ending. A first-things-first person may assume that the place to start is with the beginning. Paradoxically, the best starting point for developing a presentation is in the middle. Before you can decide how to draw an audience into your argument, you need to know exactly what the argument includes.

In *Writing for Decision Makers* (Lifetime Learning Publications, 1981), we recommend a systematic process for organizing a logical argument. Using such a system is critical in oral presentations, in which the logic of your argument is key to holding your listeners' attention. In addition, a logical system helps you limit or expand your discussion to meet the needs of a particular audience.

At this point, you have written your objective and analyzed your audience. Your next step is to establish criteria against which to measure the relative worth of alternative solutions. Although brainstorming sessions and individual research may suggest additional criteria, don't wait until you're ready to organize your material to develop criteria. Most presenters are understandably loath to give up seemingly attractive solutions once they've committed themselves to them; as a result, many people tend to bend the criteria to fit their pet solution. Developing criteria first will not only focus your problem solving, it will preserve your objectivity and improve your chances of making a convincing proposal.

Establishing Criteria

The criteria governing a decision come from several sources. The nature of an organization's mission may dictate certain standards. In most investment banks, for example, any proposed change in the organization chart must meet the test of "maximizing accountability," a standard that is far less important in an industry like advertising or publishing, where "creating substantial opportunities for creative expression" takes precedence. Most presenters develop a feel for their organization's criteria. If you're new to an organization, however, it may help to get some advice on organizational criteria from a co-worker or mentor.

The decision maker also provides criteria. Refer to your completed audience profile under the question "What is the decision maker's view of the problem?" Because the decision maker may have a broader view of the problem than you do, his or her criteria may relate to feasibility. For example, one criterion may be: "The cost of the proposed program must be allocable over the next three years." The decision maker may also have criteria that result from a personal bias. For example, he may have had a bad experience with consultants five years ago and is now inclined to say "No program can depend on outside vendors." You may decide to argue against this criterion, but you cannot ignore it. (We will consider this problem in detail as we discuss organization, order, and beginnings.)

You, as the presenter, are the person most knowledgeable about the situation. Therefore, you should have criteria based on how you perceive the problem. If you believe part of the problem is the workers' failure to take responsibility for their errors, for example, then one of your criteria might be that the new program include a system for penalizing workers for unchecked errors.

Be Specific

Once you establish the criteria on which you will base any recommendation, write them down in complete sentences and keep rewriting until they are as specific as you can make them. It's tempting to try to juggle them in your head, especially if you like to operate in the world of intuition, but only sentences that identify a specific subject and verb can be used as standards against which you can measure the value of your proposal.

As in clarifying your objective, stating criteria demands that you be precise. When asked, "What are your criteria for your next job?" most people come up with a list of words or phrases like: "salary," "location," "opportunity for advancement," "opportunity to use my skills." But these are not useful in helping someone suggest a new job. Although the person who made the list may have a fairly good idea of what he or she meant, the listener does not. For example, how much salary is enough? What geographical location do you prefer? (Is the decision between a large city and exurbia?) How fast does career advancement have to be? What opportunities for developing skills do you want the job to provide? Imprecision in formulating criteria usually reflects fuzzy thinking and eventually leads to weak support for your recommendation.

The best way to create accurate criteria is to form complete sentences that use the words "should" or "must" and include words specific enough that the problem solver or listener can actually visualize how the proposal satisfies the criteria. Using the example above, consider these criteria:

- The position must pay a salary of $35,000.
- The position must be in the Boston-Washington, D.C. corridor.
- The position must include an opportunity for a major promotion within two years.
- The position must provide an opportunity to use my analytical skills and strategic-planning background.

These are specific, workable criteria that allow you to decide among several job offers.

Once you've created full "should-must" sentences for all possible criteria, check to see whether any can be grouped together. Also be certain that compliance can be measured or evaluated. To illustrate the process of consolidating and refining criteria, let's look at the criteria a personnel director compiled for a presentation dealing with the company's promotion policy for engineers:

```
The candidate must be able to produce creative
designs.

The candidate must have intellectual ability.

The candidate must have potential to contribute to
future profits.

The candidate must have a proven track record.
```

We asked the director how he would define intellectual ability. He responded that the engineer had to have the ability to make plans work. When asked how he would know if the candidate had that ability, the director elaborated: "The engineer must be able to get jobs done on time and within the budget." We then asked how he would measure a "proven track record" and were told that it would depend on whether the candidate completed jobs on time and within the budget. We asked how he would measure the candidate's ability to contribute to future profits and got the same answer. We were then able to reduce his list to three criteria:

> The candidate must have a record of producing creative designs.
>
> The candidate must have a record of getting jobs done on time.
>
> The candidate must have a record of getting jobs done within budget.

Distinguish and Rank Criteria

Once you've narrowed down your criteria, you need to separate those your proposal *must* meet (limits of freedom) from those that are merely desirable (negotiable criteria). Limits of freedom may be budget limitations (if the budget really is firm), legal restrictions (wheelchair ramps for new construction, FTC regulations, tax rules), or perhaps generally accepted accounting procedures. In most cases, the caveat of being "consistent with company policy," although exalted in bureaucratic organizations, should not be considered a limit of freedom. Since company policy is usually a codification of criteria used in the past, and since rapid change is a condition of the 1980s, consistency is not necessarily desirable. From this perspective, let's now look at the criteria listed by the warehouse manager whose task was to choose between acquiring an in-house computer system for inventory management and contracting with a computer services company. His criteria were:

> The chosen system should cut costs of inventory management by $200,000 annually.
>
> The chosen system should improve turnaround time by an average of three days.

The chosen system should not result in layoffs.

The chosen system must be compatible with the main-frame computer at corporate headquarters.

In this listing, the first three criteria are "desirable" and, thus, negotiable; compatibility with the company's mainframe computer, however, is a "must," that is, a limit of freedom.

Deciding which criteria are most important is the presenter's responsibility. We suggest you assign each criterion a number to show its relative importance. We recommend a scale from 1 to 5 in which 5 is high. (If you employ more subdivisions than five, you create an artificial sophistication for what is really a rough measure.) Once you have assigned a rank, write down your reason for choosing that rank. (If you need to defend your decision later, your written comments will jog your memory.) The worksheet on page 202 in the appendix should be helpful.

Our warehouse manager came up with the following ranking:

Negotiable Criteria	Rank	Reason for Ranking
The chosen system should improve turnaround time by an average of three days.	5	We are losing customers because of slow turnaround time. This is our most critical problem.
The chosen system should cut costs of inventory management by $200,000 annually.	4	Our costs are far in excess of average for our industry and are hurting profits.
The chosen system should not result in layoffs.	2	We'd like to keep morale up by keeping all our employees, but cutting costs is more important.

After you have ranked your own criteria, jot down any of the decision makers' criteria you noted on your audience profile and chose
not to use in problem solving—not to guide your ultimate decision
but to consider when you develop the beginning and order your
arguments for the final presentation.

Evaluate the Alternatives

Once you have refined your criteria and jockeyed them into a
rough order, you can look critically at alternative recommendations.

One way to begin evaluating alternative proposals or recommendations is to use a trade-off worksheet like the one shown on page
36. Only negotiable criteria appear on this form. Limits of freedom
aren't listed because you have already discarded any proposal that
did not meet the essential requirements. (Limits of freedom, however, will be important later, when you make the presentation.)
Looking at one alternative at a time, each criterion is assigned a
value depending on how well the alternative meets that criterion.
For the warehouse manager, Alternative A, instituting an in-house
system, met the first criterion almost perfectly, so it was assigned a
value of 5. For the second criterion, however (to achieve a savings
of $200,000 annually), the in-house system would only save
$100,000, so the value assigned was 3. On the last criterion, the
system was assigned a value of 1 because its implementation
would result in pink slips for four workers. The same procedure
was repeated for Alternative B, using an outside contractor.

Once values have been assigned, each value is multiplied by the
criterion's rank to produce a score. The scores are added to reach a
total, which provides a rough method for comparing alternatives.
In the example, the in-house system has a score of 39; the outside
system, a score of 28. (See Exhibit 3.1 for a completed trade-off
worksheet.) These numbers do not provide legitimate quantitative
support for choosing a solution, since the weights and rankings
are subjective. They do, however, provide a technique for comparing alternatives against a number of criteria.

When you have solved the problem and know what you want to
say, you are ready to write a specific objective, review your audience profile, and organize your presentation.

Constructing an Organization Tree

At this point, you are ready to develop the logical structure of
your argument in the form of an organization tree, a form far more

TRADE-OFF WORKSHEET

Criteria	Rank	Assigned Value	Score	Reason for Value Assigned
Alternative A:				
		×	=	
		×	=	
		×	=	
	Total Score		=	
Alternative B:				
		×	=	
		×	=	
		×	=	
	Total Score		=	

useful than the traditional outline because it forces you to consider how your ideas are related to each other. When you were introduced to the outline in the fifth grade, you were encouraged to think in terms of general topics (a report on Brazil, for example, would include I. Geography; II. Political System; III. People; and so on). The tree, in contrast, guides you to examine the validity of the

Exhibit 3.1

TRADE-OFF WORKSHEET

Criteria	Rank	Assigned Value	Score	Reason for Value Assigned

Alternative A:

INSTITUTE AN IN-HOUSE EDP INVENTORY MANAGEMENT SYSTEM.

Criteria	Rank	Assigned Value	Score	Reason for Value Assigned
THE CHOSEN SYSTEM SHOULD IMPROVE TURNAROUND TIME AN AVERAGE OF THREE DAYS.	5 ×	5	= 25	CONVERSATIONS WITH OTHER USERS SAY TURNAROUND IMPROVES TWO TO FOUR DAYS.
THE CHOSEN SYSTEM SHOULD CUT INVENTORY COSTS BY $200,000 ANNUALLY.	4 ×	3	= 12	PROJECTED SAVING IS $100,000 YEARLY.
THE CHOSEN SYSTEM SHOULD NOT REQUIRE LAYOFF.	2 ×	1	= 2	WE'LL NEED TO LAY OFF FOUR WAREHOUSE WORKERS.

Total Score = 39

Alternative B:

CONTRACT WITH COMPUTER SERVICES COMPANY TO HANDLE INVENTORY MANAGEMENT.

Criteria	Rank	Assigned Value	Score	Reason for Value Assigned
THE CHOSEN SYSTEM SHOULD IMPROVE TURNAROUND TIME AN AVERAGE OF THREE DAYS.	5 ×	2	= 10	TURNAROUND IMPROVES BY ABOUT ONE DAY.
THE CHOSEN SYSTEM SHOULD CUT INVENTORY COSTS BY $200,000 ANNUALLY.	4 ×	2	= 8	PROJECTED SAVINGS ARE $80,000.
THE CHOSEN SYSTEM SHOULD NOT REQUIRE LAYOFFS.	2 ×	5	= 10	NO LAYOFFS NECESSARY.

Total Score = 28

relationships among your supporting points. While a linear outline separates major topics by large chunks of detail, a tree holds important points close together so their similarity or dissimilarity is quite visible. The tree, unlike the outline, depicts only the *body* of your presentation—beginnings and endings follow different rules, which are discussed in the next chapter.

The organization of the tree depends on the type of presentation you are going to make. For something simple, like a progress report, you can structure your presentation around the parts of your analysis. If your purpose in making the presentation is to tell the audience how to implement a course of action, the body will be organized around the steps people will have to take. If you are presenting an evaluation (that is, if your presentation focuses on the relative merits of several alternatives), you can deal with each criterion and show how each alternative meets that criterion, or you can plod through the alternatives one by one. Our preference is to deal with each criterion in turn to avoid repetition. If, however, you are making a recommendation (as you do in most management presentations), you should base the organization of your presentation on the reasons for your recommendation, each reason being derived from a statement of the way your recommendation satisfies one of your major criteria. There's a subtle difference between basing your organization on the criteria themselves (as you do in an evaluation) and basing it on reasons for the recommendation—a difference that will become clear as we continue with our example of the inventory management system.

A worksheet for preparing your organization tree is shown on page 39. To create a tree, follow these steps:

Start with the Main Point

On the far left of the tree, fill in the one concept you want the audience to remember—the Main Point. This statement will be your *recommendation* or the *overriding generalization about your analysis*. In the example we've been following, the recommendation, or Main Point, would be: "I recommend we install an in-house computer system to handle inventory management in our warehouse." (See Exhibit 3.2 for completed worksheet.)

Fill in the Major Support Points

In the center section, fill in statements serving as Major Support Points. For a presentation that recommends a course of action, all these statements are *reasons based on criteria;* for an evaluation, they are *criteria or alternatives;* for a presentation explaining an implementation plan, *steps;* for a progress report, *parts of the analysis.* Because the warehouse example involves a recommendation logically supported by reasons, each major support point must be confined to a reason, and each reason must be based on a criterion. (Compare the criteria on the trade-off worksheet, Exhibit

3.1, with the major support points on the organization tree work-sheet, Exhibit 3.2.) A point like "This system can be installed next week" would not be included because speedy installation is not one of the criteria.

Notice that the major support points apply to the *negotiable crite-ria*. The *limit of freedom* (in our example, compatibility with the existing computer) could be a major support point if the audience

ORGANIZATION TREE WORKSHEET

Main Point
(What you want
the reader
to remember)

Major Support Points
(Must relate to
the main point
in the same way)

**Detailed
Support Points**

did not know or accept it. Usually, however, since it is an accepted fact that any proposal must meet the limits of freedom, you will state them in the beginning, not in the body of the presentation. In the body, you concentrate on less obvious matters.

It is important to recognize that, most times, your recommendation will *not* fit your criteria perfectly. If your recommendation fails to meet a criterion, you'll still need to deal with that criterion in your presentation. Deliberate omissions will either leave the audience with a nagging sense that something is missing or raise questions that the presenter may not be able to handle. If the recommendation fails to satisfy a criterion, you must say so and build good support to overcome that difficulty. If, instead, the recommendation simply is not *best* on all counts, you might write:

```
An in-house system promises the fastest turnaround
time.

An in-house system saves $100,000 a year.

An in-house system involves minimal layoffs.
```

In this case, the last point does not totally support the recommendation (remember that one of the criteria was avoiding layoffs), but the phrasing suggests that this shortcoming is not damaging.

Although the sample tree in Exhibit 3.2 has only three branches for major support points, your tree may have as many branches as there are major support points for your argument (*reasons* if you're making a recommendation; *alternatives* or *criteria* for an evaluation; *important parts* for the analysis in a progress report, or *steps* in an implementation plan). Keep in mind, though, that listeners cannot retain more than seven ideas at a time. The fewer concepts you attempt to get across, the more successful you're likely to be.

Add Detailed Support Points

To the right of each branch, write statements that provide evidence for your Major Support Points. These twigs may be asser-

Exhibit 3.2

```
┌─────────────────────────────────────────────────────────────┐
│                 ORGANIZATION TREE WORKSHEET                   │
│                                                              │
│      Main Point          Major Support Points                │
│    (What you want            (Must relate to                 │
│      the reader             the main point      Detailed     │
│    to remember)            in the same way)   Support Points │
└─────────────────────────────────────────────────────────────┘
```

Main Point
(What you want
the reader
to remember)

Major Support Points
(Must relate to
the main point
in the same way)

Detailed
Support Points

AN IN-HOUSE
SYSTEM PROMISES
THE FASTEST
TURNAROUND
TIME.

I RECOMMEND
WE INSTALL
AN IN-HOUSE
COMPUTER
SYSTEM FOR
INVENTORY
MANAGEMENT.

AN IN-HOUSE
SYSTEM WILL
SAVE
$100,000
YEARLY.

AN IN-HOUSE
SYSTEM
INVOLVES
MINIMAL
LAYOFFS.

tions that require further support or they may be the findings or evidence upon which you base the subsidiary conclusions that lead to your major conclusions or recommendation. Whatever form your support takes, it must adhere to the rules of argument if it is to be persuasive. The development must be inductive, cause and effect, or deductive.

Inductive arguments. Most assertions in management presentations are grounded on inductive arguments, in which several specific statements share a common characteristic. Taken together these statements suggest a conclusion. The argument shown in Exhibit 3.2 is an inductive argument. It provides three separate reasons why the in-house system is best. Taken together, if these reasons are based on all the appropriate criteria, they represent a valid argument. Look also at Exhibit 3.3, where three characteristics of Secaucus are mentioned as reasons that would entice workers to relocate there: its temperate climate, its exquisite restaurants, and its opera house. If all these points were accurate (and if these were qualities that would attract workers to relocate), the conclusions that workers will relocate to new headquarters in Secaucus would be valid. Notice, however, that we're taking a great deal on faith. Not only would we need to back up each supporting point (on what authority can we say Secaucus has a temperate climate?), but we'd be called upon to defend our contention that these three qualities alone would entice workers to relocate. Inductive arguments are usually quite open to varying perspectives and, therefore, to different interpretations, a quality that makes them more interesting than competing forms of argument.

To test the quality of your inductive arguments on the organization tree, check to see whether there are at least two twigs for each major support point. If there is only one twig, you are either making an invalid generalization based on one example (in which case,

Exhibit 3.3
EXAMPLE OF INDUCTIVE ARGUMENT

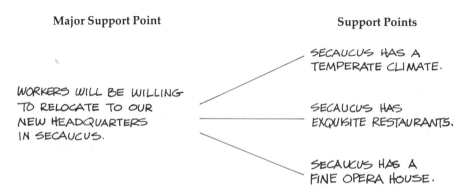

Major Support Point   Support Points

WORKERS WILL BE WILLING TO RELOCATE TO OUR NEW HEADQUARTERS IN SECAUCUS.

SECAUCUS HAS A TEMPERATE CLIMATE.

SECAUCUS HAS EXQUISITE RESTAURANTS.

SECAUCUS HAS A FINE OPERA HOUSE.

add examples or cases) or you are merely restating your major support point, which gives a false sense of development. In our example, the warehouse manager might have said:

The in-house system promises _____ The proposed system promises
the fastest turnaround time.   two-day turnaround time.

Unless the people attending the presentation know that two days is the fastest possible turnaround time to be expected from any system, a chancy assumption at best, the immediate conclusion is that the turnaround times of the outside vendors are longer. A properly developed argument would look something like this:

The in-house system we propose promises the fastest turnaround time. ⟨ The proposed system promises a two-day turnaround.
Vendor A will require three days.
Vendor B will require five days.

Cause-effect arguments. Although cause-effect arguments appear simple, they can be very tricky. When two events always occur in sequence, it's tempting to assume that one is a cause and the other an effect when, in fact, they may both be the result of another variable. A classic case of misplaced causality is the "Hawthorne Effect." Researchers at a Western Electric plant in Hawthorne, Illinois, found that a rise in production occurred when management increased the lighting in the plant. First they concluded that the poor lighting contributed to lower productivity. However, when they dramatically decreased the lighting in the plant, production again improved. The researchers concluded that it was not the degree of light but the workers' feeling that management was paying them more attention that motivated them to greater effort.

Another common error in developing these arguments is the human tendency to blame people for causing a problem when frequently the system or something in the environment is the ultimate cause. But be careful of going into the distant past for the ultimate cause. Although few people are like the labor negotiator who caustically suggested that the cause of a union's resentment was the Industrial Revolution, some managers do like to look for a long-departed culprit on which to blame today's problems.

Generally, you can check your causal arguments by determining the simplest cause and asking yourself: If we eliminate this cause, will what we want to have happen, happen? In the case shown in Exhibit 3.4, it's not clear that sprucing up Alexander Hospital's outdated obstetrical facilities alone will draw pregnant women back into the hospital. There may be a host of other factors—lack of rooming-in facilities, for example—that also contribute to the lack of patronage. Modernizing the facilities may be a necessary condition for a return to profitability through more complete use of the facilities, but it is not a sufficient condition. By asking yourself the questions on this checklist, you can strengthen your arguments.

Exhibit 3.4

Checklist for Cause-Effect Arguments

- Have I made sure that the events on which I've built my arguments are really cause and effect rather than merely correlated?
- Am I looking for a flaw in the system rather than a person to blame?
- Have I based my argument on eliminating the ultimate or necessary cause of the problem, rather than concentrating on a peripheral cause?

EXAMPLE OF CAUSE-EFFECT ARGUMENT

Major Support Point   Support Points

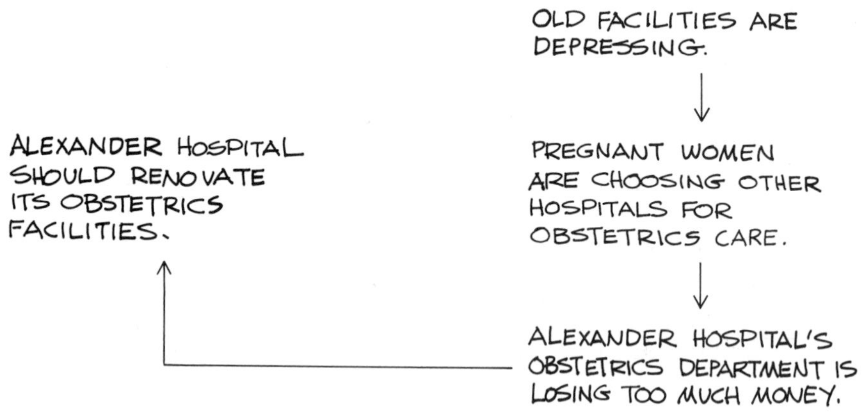

OLD FACILITIES ARE DEPRESSING.

↓

ALEXANDER HOSPITAL SHOULD RENOVATE ITS OBSTETRICS FACILITIES.

PREGNANT WOMEN ARE CHOOSING OTHER HOSPITALS FOR OBSTETRICS CARE.

↓

ALEXANDER HOSPITAL'S OBSTETRICS DEPARTMENT IS LOSING TOO MUCH MONEY.

Deductive arguments. Logic validates deductive arguments. These arguments are constructed using a major premise or general statement, a minor premise that refers to the major premise in some way, and a conclusion. (Exhibit 3.5 gives an example.) Although a legitimate form of argument, deductive arguments are seldom used in management presentations. First of all, constructing a valid deductive argument usually takes a great deal of time. For the argument presented in Exhibit 3.5, for example, you will have to spend considerable time supporting your major premise (that companies with huge debt-service burdens jeopardize their survival) because your opponents may be able to cite many examples of firms with large debt-service commitments that have survived and prospered. (By this time, your audience will be silently begging you to come to the point.) Then you will have to prove that Acme's burden is indeed huge (your minor premise) before you can reach a conclusion.

You should consider using a deductive argument only when you are dealing with a hostile audience (Acme's Board of Directors, for example, which has steadfastly refused to believe a heavy debt-service is problematic). However, even in this case, an inductive or a causal argument might be more persuasive because either tends to be more flexible and more positive.

Exhibit 3.5

EXAMPLE OF DEDUCTIVE ARGUMENT

Major Support Point   Support Points

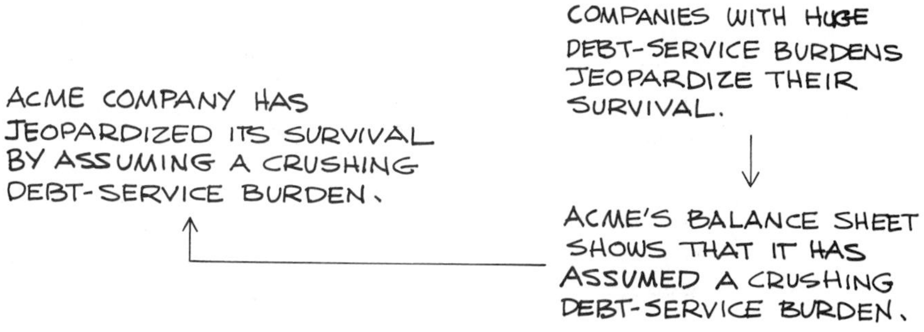

COMPANIES WITH HUGE
DEBT-SERVICE BURDENS
JEOPARDIZE THEIR
SURVIVAL.

ACME COMPANY HAS
JEOPARDIZED ITS SURVIVAL
BY ASSUMING A CRUSHING
DEBT-SERVICE BURDEN.

ACME'S BALANCE SHEET
SHOWS THAT IT HAS
ASSUMED A CRUSHING
DEBT-SERVICE BURDEN.

Develop the Supporting Evidence

The evidence in management presentations is largely statistical, just as the form of argument is usually inductive. Although managers are most comfortable with descriptive statistics (data showing *what is*), they must constantly make decisions based on incomplete information. For this reason, they frequently must accept inferential statistics (generalizing from the behavior of several members to the behavior of the whole population). Managers must constantly balance their desire for more supporting data with the need to move ahead. One of the most difficult tasks for a beginning manager is to make recommendations that do not include the request for more time to gather data. Although we are not concerned here with your research skills, we do argue for reasonableness and accuracy in data gathering (something that will become increasingly palatable with personal computers and data base management programs), and a good grasp of sampling and extrapolation principles. A wayward conclusion or a hasty generalization can undo the most carefully crafted presentation. And the ability to explain in lay terms how you got from here to there is essential to your credibility as a presenter.

Many public speaking courses list as substantiating evidence personal anecdotes, analogy, expert testimony, and quotations. Although we believe intuition and flashes of insight (on which top management often bases decisions) to be frequently as important as statistical data, such things as anecdotes are clearly not evidence. They are, rather, devices public speakers use to relieve the tedium of the after-dinner speech. Similarly, anecdotes, analogies, and quotations may occasionally find their way into your introduction as an interest-drawing device, but they are a distraction in the body of your presentation. Finally, "expert testimony" has been so abused in the legal sphere that you may find it falls flat. Authorities your audience knows and respects, however, may be effective in supporting your position as long as you use them as a source for facts rather than judgment. If you quote others, don't be glib: "Harry over in Personnel agrees with me on this." Instead, give your listeners a complete, factual statement: "I spoke with Harry Gottlieb in Personnel last week, and he confirmed that turnover has been rising in every department."

All your evidence, of whatever kind, appears on your organization tree as supporting points for your argument. Once again, although the sample tree depicted in Exhibit 3.2 shows only one set of twigs for each major support point, you must develop each argument as far as is sensible. A rule of thumb is to develop each major support point until your listeners stop asking silent questions as they assimilate the information. You may use any one of the argument forms we have discussed to support a major support branch or twig; however, all the support for any assertion must be of the same form.

Review the Structure

After you've constructed the organization tree, let it rest for a day or two, and then examine it critically.

Check all support points to make sure they are generalizations about the points to the right of them and nothing else. The advantage of using the organization tree is that it forces you to scrape your argument bare of irrelevancies (always a desirable goal but particularly so when you have only 20 to 30 minutes in which to make a point). If you've jammed in an idea simply because you've done a great deal of work on it, a dispassionate examination of the tree will reveal the fault. Drop irrelevant ideas that do not properly support the point to their left. Including them weakens your argument. On the other hand, a fresh look at the tree will help you pinpoint the places where you need additional support.

See that your support points do not overlap. Even though you checked for redundancies earlier, you may still spot an overlap after you've constructed the tree. Remember, though, that everything in the world ultimately relates to everything else, and, for this purpose, some categorization is necessary. In other words, in our sample tree (Exhibit 3.2) "cutting down turnaround time," although it may also "save money," may be important enough in itself to be a major support branch rather than a twig.

Make sure the tree reveals the criteria. If you are making a recommendation or evaluating alternatives review the list of criteria you originally developed to see if you have left out any important ones simply because they're controversial and you're afraid to deal with them. Although you may stand by your original decision not to include certain criteria, this is the time to reevaluate their significance. If you choose to ignore a criterion that is important to someone hearing the presentation, you must be prepared to explain why. Otherwise that person will become preoccupied with it. You may deal with such sticky problems by discussing these criteria at the beginning of your presentation, a tactic we talk about in the next chapter.

Checklist for Organization Tree

1. **Is the main point the one concept you want the audience to remember?** (This statement will be the recommendation or the overriding generalization about the analysis.)

2. **Do the major support points all relate to the main point in the same way?** (In a recommendation these will all be reasons based on criteria; in an evaluation of alternatives, either alternatives or criteria; in an implementation plan, steps; in a progress report, the parts of the analysis.)

3. **Do the points to the right of any assertion all relate to that assertion in the same way?**

4. **At each level of inference, does the statement generalize about the assertions to the right of it and about nothing else?**

Ordering Your Points Effectively

In deciding which points to talk about first, keep in mind that:
- People tend to trust those who agree with them
- People are more often persuaded by reasons important to them than by reasons dear to the presenter
- People stop listening and start developing counterarguments when their deeply rooted convictions are threatened.

In other words, your task is to address first those points most important to the people you most want to persuade. If you win their confidence, they will more likely hear and remember your argument. This is especially important if you believe some of your support points could be questioned—for example, in a crisis situation when you have not had time to build consensus or to do all the research you would have liked.

Once you've arrived at a final version of your tree, you are ready to decide when to make your main point and in what order to make your supporting points. Although years of writing academic papers and reading mystery stories sometimes leads people to save the main point for last, that tactic is disastrous for a management presentation. First, management audiences are not interested in second-guessing you; they want answers quickly. Second, people will understand your argument better if they know the direction in which you are leading them. Third, you should take advantage of the fact that people remember best what they hear first and last. Tell them what you want them to know twice—once when you start and once when you finish. The only time you should consider saving the recommendation or conclusion for the last is if the audience will not give your point of view a fair hearing. In that case, you may need to build your case argument by argument until the audience has no choice but to accept your conclusion. In such a situation, first discuss the arguments you know the audience will support, that is, those that provoke the least controversy. If your presentation focuses on an evaluation of various alternatives, the best order is either from most to least advantageous or from least to most controversial.

For other presentations, the choices are obvious. As Exhibit 3.6 shows, if the audience's main question in a recommendation pre-

Exhibit 3.6

HOW TO ORDER SUPPORTING POINTS

Type of Presentation	Implicit Question	Elements of the Argument	Suggested Order
Recommendation	What should we do?	Reasons based on criteria	Most-to-least important Least-to-most controversial
Evaluation	What are my choices?	Criteria or alternatives	Most-to-least advantageous
Progress report	What is the status?	Details of the analysis	Most-to-least important
		Stages in the process	Sequential
Implementation	How should we do it?	Steps in the process	Sequential

sentation is: What should we do? your argument structure will be based on reasons ordered chronologically or progressively from most to least important. Progress reports are based on a parts-of-the-whole structure and require a logical order from most to least important or from largest to smallest. Finally, if the task is to explain how something works or how people should proceed, your structure will look remarkably like a flow chart and will progress in sequence.

Learn about Other Structures.

Although these structures and orders are appropriate for the vast majority of management presentations, you should be familiar with other forms in case you encounter them as a listener or need them in specialized situations.

Pro-and-con structure. Many former debaters are reluctant to let go of the pro-and-con format. In this structure, you state all the points in favor, balance them with all the points against, and conclude that one position outweighs the other. One presenter made these notes for a short presentation to her boss who had asked her to find an alternative slide supplier.

```
GRAPHIC PLUS

Pros
   Accuracy:          Laser plotter provides sharper graphs
                      and charts
   Colors:            More choices
   Charts:            2,300 including maps
   Location:          Close to downtown

Cons
   Delivery:          Each pickup costs $17.50
   Service charges:   More than current supplier
   Cost per slide:    $2.25 more than current supplier
   Turnaround time:   Very slow compared to current supplier

CONCLUSION
   Stay with current supplier
```

Even though the presenter believed she was being persuasive by compiling all the positive and negative features of Graphic Plus, her argument was not compelling because she did not compare Graphic Plus to the existing supplier in each case. Furthermore, her notes did not indicate the importance of each feature. One of the major disadvantages in the pro-and-con structure is the absence of precise, thoughtfully ranked criteria.

Process-of-elimination structure. Another structure you may encounter in management presentations is referred to as the process of elimination. Presenters adopt this structure for two reasons: First, it takes little time to deliver; second, although potentially dangerous, it can be persuasive. Here's an example:

```
You have only three alternatives to save your investment
in this business: (1) sell the company, (2) diversify
through acquisition or (3) market your product more
aggressively.

The facts are that you can't sell the company (no one
will buy it), and you can't diversify (you don't have
the capital).

THEREFORE, you must aggressively market your product.
```

The process-of-elimination structure is valid and economical, but it works only if you have identified all possible alternatives and really eliminated all but one. It's extraordinarily difficult to meet these two tests, particularly if you're dealing with any complex issue. Although some people like the shock value of this technique, in most instances, the audience will view this structure as presumptuous because of its implication that your final recommendation must be accepted.

The "Yes, but . . ." structure. The "yes, but . . ." structure is a two-part argument in which the presenter builds an apparently strong case for the proposal the audience prefers and then destroys it by showing a fault in one of the essential points. Organizing this kind of argument is something like building a table with a trick leg. You agree with the audience about the elegance and sturdiness of the table and then expose the defective leg.

For example, a manager disagreed with her audience's position on how to cover the company's long-term debt. The decision makers wanted to refinance using a sophisticated debt instrument. The presenter explained how this option would initially result in a tremendous jump in the price of their stock (something they obviously wanted) and pointed out other benefits. She concluded, however, by noting that the ratio of current debt to current assets would violate the company's covenant with other lenders (the trick leg), and that lowering the ratio through other means was not feasible. Because building support for an option only to destroy it is extremely frustrating to an audience, use this structure with caution.

Thesis-antithesis-synthesis structure. In this classic three-part argument, the presenter first states and supports the case for one alternative, then states and supports the case for its opposite, and finally presents a proposal combining the most desirable parts of both. For negotiations, and for those rare audiences that include two diametrically opposed factions, this structure may work. By presenting each faction's view in the beginning without bias, you acknowledge its position and create trust.

In one corporation, for example, the human relations department had traditionally participated in all hiring decisions. A new vice-president insisted that the result was the employment of a large number of people who "couldn't cut the mustard." He wrote a policy memo eliminating this review for positions at top staff levels. When the head of the human relations department and her staff protested, the vice-president asked his executive assistant to present a scenario for negotiation. The assistant used the thesis-antithesis-synthesis approach and was successful in arriving at a recommendation that both the vice-president and the human relations department could accept.

When using this form of argument, talk to proponents of both sides to test your understanding of the thesis and antithesis and to see the merits of both positions. Both sides will then know they can trust you. In presenting an issue from two diametrically opposed points of view, you also sharpen your logical and intellectual skills.

All of these alternate forms have a common failing: The main point is delayed rather than announced soon after the presenter begins to speak. For most management presentations, although you may generate some anticipatory excitement by holding off, it's far better to arouse and hold interest through the power of your argument, your delivery skills, and your polished visuals.

Now that you have your argument in order, you can go on to designing the presentation as a whole.

SUMMARY

Logic is essential if a management presentation is to be persuasive. To construct a logical argument for the body of your presentation, you must:
- Establish and rank criteria
  —be specific and concrete
  —determine which criteria are most important
- Evaluate alternatives
- Construct an organization tree
  —write out the main point, the one thing you want the audience to remember
  —develop the major supporting points, which will be reasons based on criteria, criteria or alternatives, steps, or parts of the analysis
  —provide detailed support in the form of inductive, deductive, or cause-effect arguments
- Choose a persuasive order
  —give the main point first
  —order the supporting arguments logically
- Learn about other structures
  —the pro-and-con structure
  —the process-of-elimination structure
  —the "Yes, but . . ." structure
  —the thesis-antithesis-synthesis structure

4

DESIGNING THE
PRESENTATION

To convert a tight argument into a persuasive presentation,
- Craft an appropriate beginning and ending
- Make storyboards to synthesize the elements into a coherent whole
  —insure effective transitions
  —determine the best place for visual support
  —check presentation length
  —prepare for questions

Up to this point, developing an oral presentation has been much the same as developing a written one. You have determined your objective, analyzed your audience, constructed an organization tree, and ordered your main points. Now, before you begin to put the parts together, you should take into account the differences between readers and listeners. Unlike readers, your listeners are totally dependent on you, the presenter, for focus. They have only one opportunity to grasp your message. They cannot reread or look ahead in the text for clues, and they cannot drift off into fantasy and hope to pick up the argument later. Therefore, you need to use techniques that hold their attention. A compelling beginning, an action-oriented ending, and an effective blending of words and visual support are the components of a smooth presentation.

Crafting the Beginning

The beginning of a presentation prepares the audience to receive and understand your argument. It may be long or short, depending on how much your listeners know about the subject, what their preconceptions are, and what your relationship with them is. In addition, because they have all left another activity to attend your presentation, they are more likely to be thinking about something important to them than about your topic. Creating a beginning that compels an audience to concentrate on your subject requires that you carefully select what you say and how you say it.

What Goes into a Beginning

A good beginning is one that interests the audience and sets the stage for the rest of the presentation. To do this, it must include WHAT the presentation is about and WHY it is important, establish rapport with the audience, and show HOW your argument will be developed.

State the subject and its importance. People will settle down and concentrate on your presentation only if you convince them there is something in it for them or, by extension, for the organization. Most managers believe unfocused meetings and presentations make it more difficult for them to get their work done. For instance, if the department budget is due next week, including in a presentation a detailed discussion of the theory behind management training programs, even if those programs are included in the budget, will seem like a terrible waste of time. Therefore, a presenter who begins by saying, "John asked me to discuss our new training program," will not cause many decision makers to stop thinking about columns of budget figures, even if John is the CEO. On the other hand, consider this opening:

> As the result of John's mandate to eliminate 10 percent of our managerial positions within the next three years, we will need to increase the productivity of all remaining managers. We can do that only if they are trained to take on additional responsibility.

This statement makes the connection between the management training program and the budget quite clear.

It is also difficult for your listeners to concentrate on your subject if they don't know specifically what the subject is. In other words, if you say, "Today I'm going to tell you about computerized inventory systems," they won't listen. No one in the room is interested in a generic discussion. Everyone knows you have a purpose, and they want to know what it is. In most instances, it is best to state your recommendation directly:

> We should institute a computerized inventory management system by 1987 because it will save $40,000 a quarter.

Listeners generally appreciate having your final recommendation up front. They then know where you're headed and can follow the logic of your argument better. In those rare instances when you have to lead up to a recommendation or risk the audience rejecting it out of hand, you must still be specific about the subject.

> In deciding whether or not a computerized inventory management system would be effective, we must consider potential changes in turnaround time, cost savings, and initial price. Today, I'll discuss each of these in turn.

If you are to get and hold your audience's attention, you must, within the first few minutes of your presentation, indicate specifically what you will discuss and why it is important to everyone in the room.

Establish rapport with your audience. Members of an audience respond more positively to a speaker whom they trust and whom they perceive to be an expert. If you know the members of the audience and they understand why you're making the presentation, you won't need to establish your credentials. If, however, the audience doesn't know you or is likely to oppose your ideas, you, or the person introducing you, must make sure that your expertise is conveyed to the audience.

Before the presentation begins, discuss the introduction with the person who will introduce you. Introductions are usually much too long. No one is interested in an exhaustive recital of monographs you've written or a detailed discussion of your career. But an audience will respond to a simple statement like:

> Susan Thomas is a member of our legal staff. She has several recommendations concerning the company's affirmative action program based on her review of the impact of the new law.

If you're introducing yourself, you can use the same approach:

> I'm Samuel White of the Legal Department. I've reviewed the new affirmative action law in detail and want to discuss with you four areas in which compliance is important.

Most people find it difficult to state their own credentials because they believe such statements make them appear arrogant. Yet there's an enormous difference between starting out with, "I am completely familiar with this topic," which suggests you think you know everything, and saying, "I have reviewed. . . ." The first is a statement of opinion; the other a statement of fact. Far from making you seem arrogant, statements of fact make you appear knowledgeable and self-confident, two important qualities in establishing rapport.

It is not enough, however, to be an expert. People trust speakers who understand their point of view. In preparing your beginning, check your audience profile to see whether any members of the audience are likely to reject all or part of your argument and whether you have ignored any criteria that may be important to them. In dealing with a potentially antagonistic audience, make it clear to your listeners that you understand their position. For example, you might say:

> I know you are concerned principally with the cost of any program we undertake. Although cost is important, because of our backlog of orders it is vital that we give primary consideration to training our workers on the new equipment.

In addition, because your purpose is to arrive at a common perspective on the problem, state why you chose your criteria. If you don't, the audience is likely to worry about your apparent lack of understanding when they should be focusing on your logic.

Provide guidelines for the discussion. A good beginning must also alert the audience to the way you intend to develop your presentation. Opening guidelines are akin to the table of contents or the executive summary of a written report. Without them, the audience will struggle along wondering what direction you will take next and when you will finish. If your listeners can mentally check off your points as you make them, they will be able to focus on your argument more easily.

Some presenters believe they are providing guidelines when they say, "I will talk about four things today." They then proceed to the first item, and create a transition by saying, "That's the first point. My second point is . . ." Although this approach sets boundaries for the listeners, it does not help them follow the flow of the argument. A better approach is to use your major support points as guidelines:

> We should hold our annual meeting away from headquarters for three reasons. First, off-premises meetings produce better problem solving. Second, our staff needs the break an enforced trip entails. Finally, we need to bring our new executives together in a relaxed setting. Let's look at these arguments one by one.

After hearing this beginning, the audience knows the skeleton of the argument and, for the remainder of the presentation, each person can listen for these major points.

Confine yourself to relevant information. You will notice that, so far, we have not mentioned a standard component of many beginnings—the background of the problem. That's because, most times, the discussion of background is superfluous. A beginning should include only what the audience needs to know to understand and follow your argument. Consult your audience profile to assess the audience's knowledge of the subject. Then look at your organization tree to determine whether you've assumed too much technical expertise or experience in any of your support points. Rather than filling the beginning with detail, provide whatever is needed to understand a point at the time you discuss that point. If the audience needs general information about past experience with a situation or problem, then include a limited discussion of the history in the beginning, but be conservative.

Nothing puts an audience to sleep faster than a rehash of information everyone already knows.

Guidelines for an Effective Beginning

- State the subject and its importance
- Establish rapport with your audience
- Provide guidelines for the discussion
- Confine yourself to relevant information

Jotting down your ideas on a worksheet like the one on page 61 will help you decide what to include in your beginning. Your next concern is organizing the elements.

How to Organize Your Beginning

Audiences make judgments about speakers within the first few minutes of a presentation. If you bore or antagonize your listeners with your opening remarks, you will have trouble changing their perception of you during the remainder of the presentation. If you fail to make members of the audience concentrate on what you are saying immediately, you may never regain their attention. Therefore, your opening remarks and the way you present them are critical.

Good opening statements. If you have not been introduced, you must, of course, introduce yourself. After the "Hello, I'm ____ ," then what? Here are some good opening statements:

A statement of why the presentation is important to the audience. For example, you might say, "We can increase net earnings as much as two percent by adding a line of low-calorie lemon soda."

A statement about the audience's concerns. If you expect opposition, you may build rapport by opening with a comment that indicates you understand the audience's position.

A question soliciting the audience's concerns. A question can be an effective beginning in a small group. The drawback to this approach is that it commits you to considering all the topics your listeners may bring up. In other words, use this technique only when you know the issues the audience will raise and are prepared to discuss them all.

A statement of your qualifications. If no one has presented your qualifications and if the audience is hostile, this approach can help you establish rapport.

WORKSHEET FOR DEVELOPING A BEGINNING

What is this presentation about? (This answer should be your recommendation or conclusion, the main point of your organization tree.)

Why is this presentation important to my audience? (This statement should describe what went wrong, what may go wrong, or what opportunity exists. It may help to ask yourself "What will happen if my proposal is not accepted?")

How will I develop the argument? (List your major support points, which constitute the body of your presentation.)

What must the audience know to understand the argument? (Check your organization tree with the audience profile in mind. Does the audience need any further information about the problem? Are there criteria that must be mentioned?)

Weak opening statements. Many speech openings suggest "I will speak, you will listen" or, in an attempt to be catchy, risk boring or irritating the audience. Here are some openings to avoid.

A dramatic forecast of doom. "Your current strategy of diversification will guarantee bankruptcy within two years." Exaggerated statements like this will attract attention, but they may arouse hostility, at least among those members of the audience who helped construct the strategy you are attacking. Skip the theatrics unless you are certain the audience is predisposed to accept your idea. If you do choose to begin this way, always follow up with a solution before you take a deep breath.

A personal experience. "The other day I was talking to George and we agreed that our inventory . . ." or "The other day it took me five hours to get a count of the lumber in Warehouse 3." No one in the audience cares about what you did. Concentrate on the problem instead.

A rhetorical question. "Do you know how long it takes to get a count of the lumber in Warehouse 3?" A rhetorical question snidely suggests that the presenter knows something the audience doesn't know but should—not a good way to establish rapport. In addition, once in a while someone actually tries to answer a rhetorical question, creating an embarrassing moment for everyone.

An overworked quotation. "As Ben Franklin said, 'A penny saved is a penny earned.' We can save and earn $40,000 a quarter by computerizing . . ." Beginning with a quotation makes your presentation seem more literary than managerial, and a tired maxim like the one just mentioned insults the audience's intelligence.

A joke. We all love humor. Unfortunately, not only do most planned jokes sound contrived, they are often funny only at someone else's expense. If you aren't a professional stand-up comic, don't plan on using jokes.

An apology. "Time didn't permit me to do the kind of research I would have liked." Instead of gaining the audience's sympathy, such excuses alienate and irritate. "Poormouthing" at any point in a presentation is ill-advised—as an opening line it can be fatal. If you haven't done your homework, you are not an expert. Why should anyone listen to you?

A definition. Dictionary definitions, "Webster's defines *oligopoly* as . . ." remind everyone of elementary school reports.
In a management setting, starting with a definition is not only boring, it is condescending.

How to follow the opening statement. If, in your opening statement, you haven't told the audience what the presentation is about and why it's important, do so next. Keep in mind that an audience will remember best what you say first and what you say last. Don't waste the first few moments. Next, if you are concerned about your rapport with members of the audience, work to build their confidence by stating your criteria or responding to theirs. You can then make a natural transition into the body of the presentation by concluding the beginning with guidelines for how you will proceed.

Creating an Ending

The ending of a presentation provides a last opportunity to persuade the audience and reach agreement on the course of action. Any presenter, therefore, is well-advised to take a few minutes at the end of a presentation to:
- Repeat the recommendation or conclusion
- Set out the steps required for action

You may also want to reiterate the major support points, especially if members of the audience will have to summarize for others who could not attend, and restate the importance of the subject, emphasizing the action that is necessary. The amount of material you include in an ending depends on the audience's commitment to your position—the more committed the audience, the less you need to say.

Making Storyboards

If you were writing a report, you would, at this point, begin to write the first draft. In developing an oral presentation, the storyboards serve as the first draft. They provide a mechanism for developing transitions, checking the flow of the argument, and designing rough visuals to support your argument. If you are developing a team presentation or if a group has done the work leading up to the presentation, storyboards provide a good vehicle for reaching agreement on the text and the visuals.

Storyboard

Thesis Statement:

Supporting Statements: | Data: Charts, Tables

Transition Sentence:

Storyboards are developed from your organization tree and your worksheet for the beginning. (Exhibits 4.1–4.6 show how the process works.) Initially these storyboards are nothing more than notes to yourself. You may later want to use clean storyboards for your presentation, making sure they include transition sentences as well as the thesis statement and support for each point in the presentation. (A thesis statement is the main idea on each story-board. It may be a major support point, a support point or, in a long report, a detail that is supported with further details.) For example, you want to recommend to the beverage division of Circus Products that the company market a decaffeinated soft drink. Your argument appears on your organization tree (Exhibit 4.1). You and the other managers in the division have been talking informally about this idea for some time. There is general agreement that it is a good idea if you can prove that the market has room for another product and that you can fill that market niche effectively. Your worksheet for developing a beginning (Exhibit 4.2) suggests that you have the needed rapport with your audience and that everyone knows the fundamentals.

Now you begin to develop storyboards. You decide to approach the decision with a sense of urgency, since the idea has been kicking around for awhile and people may be tired of it. On your first storyboard, then, you begin by stating the importance of the subject in the context of the whole organization (Exhibit 4.3): "Our company's impressive record of annual volume and earnings growth is endangered by the recession and our lack of new product entries over the last five years." Because someone in the audience may question the validity of this statement, you add these supporting points:

- Our economists expect that spending on consumer package goods will continue to decline over the next several years.
- Our competitors' new products are already eroding our market share.

If you choose to support these statements with visuals, sketch them in the right-hand column.

When you make these statements during the presentation, your audience should silently ask, What should we do? Be prepared to answer with your recommendation, but first provide a transition: (Exhibit 4.3), "This erosion need not continue." This statement leads to your next storyboard (Exhibit 4.4) on which you state your main point (that is, your recommendation), "We can reestablish our reputation in the refreshment beverage market and increase ongoing net earnings by 8% if we market a decaffeinated soft drink." You then support this thesis statement with two points:

- We can increase our national beverage sales 12% in the first 24 months.
- Marketing and variable production costs will be our only entry costs.

You'll need to support each of these points later with solid evidence, but by stating them now you provide guidelines for your audience. The transition into your argument may be simply, "Let's take these one at a time." Now you can move to the main body of your presentation. Use the storyboards to present the support point and details of your argument. Exhibits 4.5 and 4.6 show support for two different pieces of the presentation. Exhibit 4.5 shows the storyboard for the first twig on the organization tree. It sup-

Exhibit 4.1
ORGANIZATION TREE

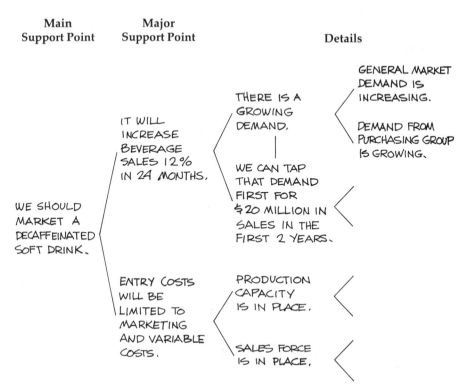

ports the assertion that the proposal will increase beverage sales 12 percent in 24 months by detailing the growing demand for decaffeinated beverages. Exhibit 4.6 shows the support for the contention that the only entry costs will be marketing and variable production costs.

Developing Transitions

Transitions are critical in management presentations not only because they link sections and emphasize relationships but also because they sum up what's already been said and forecast the next section. Judicious reviewing signals the conclusion of a major portion of the argument. Repetition increases the likelihood that the audience will remember your ideas. Transition words and phrases like "however," "therefore," "as you can see," and "in conclusion" guide the listeners through your argument. If done well, a transition can provide subliminal cues that add to the persuasive power of your presentation. Be sure, however, that you use transition words correctly. If you say "however," the audience expects an

Exhibit 4.2

WORKSHEET FOR DEVELOPING A BEGINNING

What is this presentation about? (This answer should be your recommendation or conclusion, the main point of your organization tree.)

> WE SHOULD MARKET A DECAFFEINATED
> SOFT DRINK.

Why is this presentation important to my audience? (This statement should describe what went wrong, what may go wrong, or what opportunity exists. It may help to ask yourself "What will happen if my proposal is not accepted?")

> OUR MARKET IS ERODING.
> WE CAN REESTABLISH REPUTATION AND
>   INCREASE EARNINGS.

How will I develop the argument? (List your major support points, which constitute the body of your presentation.)

> POTENTIAL FOR 12% SALES INCREASE IN
>   TWO YEARS.
> LOW COST OF ENTRY.

What must the audience know to understand the argument? (Check your organization tree with the audience profile in mind. Does the audience need any further information about the problem? Are there criteria that must be mentioned?)

> THE PROBLEM HAS BEEN AROUND FOR SOME TIME.
>   THE AUDIENCE WILL ACCEPT CRITERIA OF
>   INCREASED SALES AND LOW COSTS.

---

opposing view. "Therefore" indicates that what you are about to say follows from what you just said. If you misuse these words (and many do) you'll confuse the audience.

Spread the storyboards out on a table or pin them to a wall and read through them to see whether your argument flows smoothly. Although you checked the organization tree for logic and deter-

Exhibit 4.3

Storyboard

Thesis Statement:
OUR COMPANY'S IMPRESSIVE RECORD OF ANNUAL VOLUME AND
EARNINGS GROWTH IS ENDANGERED BY THE RECESSION AND OUR
LACK OF NEW PRODUCT ENTRIES OVER THE LAST FIVE YEARS.

Supporting Statements:

OUR ECONOMISTS EXPECT THAT SPENDING
ON CONSUMER PACKAGE GOODS WILL
CONTINUE TO DECLINE OVER THE NEXT
SEVERAL YEARS.

OUR COMPETITORS' NEW PRODUCTS
ARE ALREADY ERODING OUR
MARKET SHARE.

Data: Charts, Tables

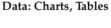

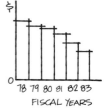

78 79 80 81 82 83
FISCAL YEARS

SHARE OF REFRESHMENT
BEVERAGE MARKET
IN TEST AREAS

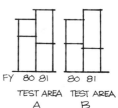

FY 80 81   80 81
TEST AREA   TEST AREA
A   B

Transition Sentence: THIS EROSION NEED NOT CONTINUE.

mined an order before you designed the storyboards, formulating
transitions may suggest changes, particularly in the order of your
argument. Now is the time to make these changes.

Determining the Best Place for Visuals

As you create your storyboards, make a rough sketch of the visuals you'll need on the boards themselves. During the problem-
solving process, you may have made rough charts and graphs.
Look at your argument with a fresh eye now and consider which
of these help make your point. Sketch new ones as needed.
Remember, you are making an audiovisual presentation, not a

Exhibit 4.4

Storyboard

Thesis Statement:

WE CAN REESTABLISH OUR REPUTATION IN THE REFRESHMENT
BEVERAGE MARKET AND INCREASE NET EARNINGS BY 8%
IF WE MARKET A DECAFFEINATED SOFT DRINK.

Supporting Statements:	**Data: Charts, Tables**
WE CAN INCREASE OUR NATIONAL BEVERAGE SALES BY 12% IN THE FIRST 24 MONTHS. MARKETING AND VARIABLE PRODUCTION COSTS WILL BE OUR ONLY ENTRY COSTS.	

Transition Sentence: LET'S TAKE THESE ONE AT A TIME.

major motion picture. Visuals should support your argument; they
should not complicate it. Use visuals only where they are needed.
That is, use charts and graphs to express a point pictorially and
text visuals to reinforce an argument, to summarize or to make a
transition.

Checking the Presentation Length

Storyboards also help you fit your presentation into the allotted
time. Although you won't know precisely the length of each section until you rehearse, you can get a rough estimate by talking

Exhibit 4.5

Storyboard

Thesis Statement:

THERE IS A GROWING DEMAND FOR DECAFFEINATED BEVERAGES.

Supporting Statements:

CONSUMER TRACKING STUDIES
INDICATE AN INCREASING INTEREST
IN DECAFFEINATED BEVERAGES.

WOMEN 18-34, WHO COMPRISE THE
LARGEST PURCHASING GROUP FOR
REFRESHMENT BEVERAGES, SHOW A
MARKED INCREASE IN INTEREST IN
BUYING DECAFFEINATED SOFT DRINKS
FOR THEMSELVES AND THEIR FAMILIES.

Data: Charts, Tables

Q: WOULD YOU TRY

TOTAL POPULATION SAMPLE

	'79	'80	'81
Y	25%	35%	59%
N	37	29	20
DN	38	36	21

Q:

WOMEN 18-34

Y

N

DN

Transition Sentence: WITH NO ONE ELSE IN THE BUSINESS, WE CAN
TRANSLATE THAT DEMAND INTO
$20 MILLION IN SALES.

---

your way through the storyboards and timing yourself. Then, as a
rule of thumb, add 10 percent more time for manipulating visuals,
responding to questions, and dealing with the usual interruptions.
Be certain, also, to leave adequate time for discussion.

When you've cut your presentation to the appropriate length,
mark the sections you can eliminate should your time be cut by
one-half or three-quarters. We know one presenter who is always
ready to cut his presentation to five minutes. If the decision maker
is called away or an earlier discussion takes longer than you

Exhibit 4.6

Storyboard

Thesis Statement:

OUR COSTS OF ENTRY WILL BE LIMITED TO MARKETING
AND VARIABLE PRODUCTION COSTS.

Supporting Statements:	Data: Charts, Tables
OUR EXISTING PRODUCTION CAPACITY CAN ACCOMMODATE ANTICIPATED DEMAND FOR A NEW PRODUCT FOR THE NEXT TWO YEARS.	CAPACITY IN GALLONS PROJECTED DEMAND IN GALLONS
OUR SALES FORCE IS ALREADY ACTIVE IN THE MARKET.	

Transition Sentence: WITH SUCH HIGH POTENTIAL AND LOW COST, WE
SHOULD MOVE AHEAD WITH MARKET TESTS.

expected, you need to be prepared to leave material out. If you are not, you are liable to make poor decisions—eliminating the wrong material or rushing through too fast.

Preparing for Questions

As you read through the storyboards, anticipate questions the listeners may ask, and list them. Then answer them for yourself and provide supporting visuals if you can. You can more easily second-guess the audience the first time you read the storyboards than when you rehearse because your argument is still fresh in your mind. (You can always add to the list if questions occur to you later.) Only when you are satisfied with the storyboards should you design the final visuals, the subject of the next chapter.

SUMMARY

Beginnings and endings are critical because audiences are most alert during the first minutes and final minutes of a presentation.
- Your beginning must tell the audience
  —WHAT the presentation is about
  —WHY the subject is important
  —HOW you will develop the argument
- If you have chosen to ignore criteria important to the audience in the body of the presentation, you must deal with them in the beginning
- An effective ending repeats the recommendation and reinforces the need for action

Storyboards provide a valuable tool, particularly for long presentations and team efforts
- Storyboards force you to write transitions and check the flow of the argument
- If your presentation is the result of a team effort, storyboards enable you to get agreement on the final version of the presentation
- Sketching rough visuals on storyboards shows you when you need to collect more data and insures even development of visual support
- Talking through the storyboards will give you a first check on the length of the presentation

5
DESIGNING AND USING VISUALS

For many people, well-designed visuals are the hallmark of a professional presentation. To design and use visuals skillfully means:

- Choosing the most appropriate medium
- Applying good design strategies
- Mastering the mechanics of making and using overheads, flipcharts, and slides

Choosing the Appropriate Medium

For most presentations, managers use transparencies, flipcharts, or 35mm slides, in roughly that order. (Although some conference rooms are furnished with a blackboard, most management presenters regard the chalk talk as too informal or too academic for anything but pure problem-solving situations.) For very elaborate presentations they may use more than one medium. In addition, managers are increasingly relying upon personal computers to play "what if?" games during the presentation itself. Your choice of medium will be influenced by the purpose of your presentation, the conventions of your industry and organization, the size of the audience, and the available resources. This choice, in turn, will influence the design of your visual aids.

The purpose of your presentation. Sometimes choosing the appropriate medium is simply a matter of common sense. If you're meeting with your boss to convince her that your budget should be approved, you wouldn't set up a projector and put on a slide show in her office. On the other hand, if you're trying to persuade the board of directors that a major expansion program is vital, you wouldn't appear in the boardroom with rough, hand-lettered flipcharts. If you make a formal presentation in an informal situation, you are liable to look self-serving and possibly dishonest. In the same way, if you saunter into the boardroom and make a few casual remarks on a critical topic, you'll look unprofessional and unprepared.

The type of visuals required to make a persuasive argument, given your purpose, will help you determine the appropriate medium. Because your audience sees flipcharts exactly as they are drawn, only the simplest charts and graphs are appropriate. If your material is at all complex, you'll need transparencies, which are enlarged when projected onto a screen. If photographs are essential to your point, you'll probably use slides. (Copying a photograph onto a transparency is generally unsatisfactory.)

The conventions in the industry and in your organization. Some industries and organizations require more formality than others. In very general terms, managers in a more mature industry, such as auto manufacturing, are more likely to expect formal presentations than are managers in an emerging industry, such as computer software, in which traditions have not been established. Consultants expect to put on a polished presentation with professionally done artwork (after all, their presentation is part of their product). In contrast, venture capitalists expect to sit around a table, rub elbows, and negotiate.

The norms of the organization also affect your choice of visuals. In organizations in which the prevailing attitude is "we're-all-in-this-together," creative, informal presentations are encouraged. In organizations with rigid hierarchies, on the other hand, presentations usually follow a detailed format, which may be preserved in a bound procedure book.

The size of your audience. Audience size also influences the visual medium you choose, simply because everyone in the audience must be able to see the visuals clearly. If the audience exceeds twenty people, for example, flipcharts are useless. Overhead transparencies (as long as they are designed correctly, the screen is large enough, and the screen and projector are appropriately set up) can be used with groups of about one hundred. For audiences of several hundred people, slides are necessary. If you have any question about legibility, experiment with a sample flipchart, overhead, or slide and station yourself as far away as a member of your audience might reasonably be expected to sit.

The available resources. Time, money, and the availability of equipment will also influence your decision. Slides, for example, take at least a day to produce and are expensive. Although amateur photographers can make slides, management audiences expect professional-looking products. Unless you have expertise in this area, send your artwork to an outside studio. You can make overheads on an office copier instantly and inexpensively by using a typed or hand-drawn original on letter-size paper. Although professionally made overheads are superior, do-it-yourself overheads are usually acceptable if they are neat. Flipcharts are easy to make yourself and are the least expensive choice. If you have them professionally drawn, the time and cost factors increase. Choose the medium in which you can produce the most professional visual given your resources—it's better, for instance, when the audience is small, to have neatly lettered flipcharts than amateurish slides.

Guidelines for Selecting a Visual Medium

Considerations	Flipcharts	Overheads	Slides
Audience size	Under 20 people	About 100 people	Several hundred people
Degree of formality	Informal	Informal or formal	Formal
Design complexity	Simple	Simple; can be made on office copier	Anything that can be photographed
Equipment and room requirements	Easel and chart	Projector and screen; shades to block light	Projector and screen; dim lighting
Production time	Drawing time only	Drawing or typing time; may be copied instantly	Design and photographing time plus at least 24 hours production time
Cost	Inexpensive unless professionally drawn	Inexpensive unless professionally designed or typeset	Relatively expensive

Applying Good Design Strategies

In their presentations, managers use both text and graphic visuals to reinforce their main points and to help the audience follow the flow of their arguments. Regardless of the type of visual, the guiding principles for an effective strategy are (1) keep it simple and (2) focus attention on your message.

Text Visuals

Text visuals (visuals that include words alone) are used primarily as road maps. They serve to preview material, summarize material, and remind the audience where you are in the presentation. (See Exhibit 5.1 for an example of a text visual.) Although a text

Exhibit 5.1
TEXT VISUALS OUTLINE THE PRESENTATION.

The proposed strategy will . . .

- Establish our corporate identity

- Improve profitability

- **Strengthen our financial condition**

- Improve our competitive position

visual may also be used to emphasize a main point, most presenters consider pictures more powerful than lines of printed text (for example, compare Exhibits 5.2 and 5.3) and use graphic examples whenever possible.

To design effective text visuals, keep in mind that the concepts must be easily grasped, and the design must be simple. Because the human eye can take in about forty characters in one glance, no line should contain more than that. And because you want to give the audience time to read without ruining your pace, four to six short lines is plenty. Use phrases rather than full sentences, expanding on each phrase as you speak.

To insure that the visual is easy to read, use upper and lower case letters. For the same reason, choose a simple typeface (clean letters are easier to recognize than ornate ones). Use bullets or Arabic numerals to set off items in a list because they are easier to read than letters or Roman numerals. If there is no sequential order to the list, bullets are preferable.

Consistency and open space help the audience focus on your message. By starting the text at the same place on all your visuals

Exhibit 5.2
A TEXT VISUAL CAN EMPHASIZE AN IMPORTANT POINT . . .

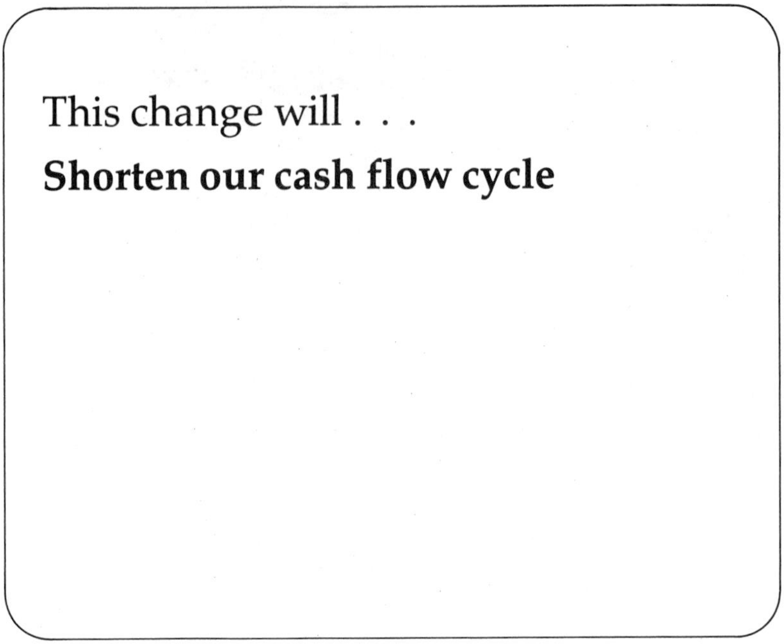

This change will . . .

Shorten our cash flow cycle

Exhibit 5.3
BUT A GRAPHIC VISUAL HAS GREATER IMPACT.

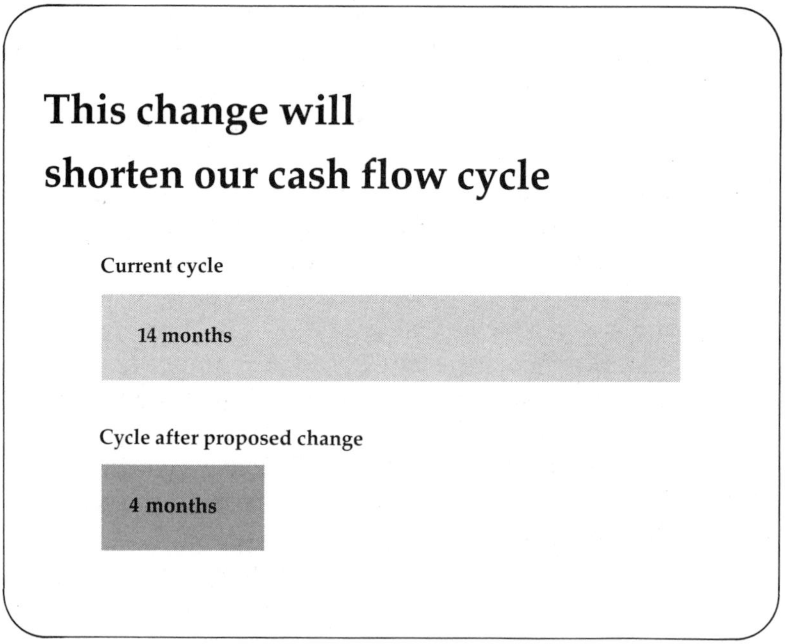

This change will
shorten our cash flow cycle

Current cycle

14 months

Cycle after proposed change

4 months

(about one-fifth of the distance from the top of the visual) and by leaving a space about the height of a capital letter between each line, people in the audience will not have to search for a starting place each time a new visual appears.

Using color, boldface, or large-sized type for important concepts helps to distinguish them from supporting ideas. By using the same feature each time you make a similar point, you can reinforce your message. For example, you can use the same text visual several times to remind the audience of your place in the argument, highlighting your location each time with one of those features as you move through the presentation (note the boldface type in Exhibit 5.1).

Guidelines for Designing Text Visuals

- Use no more than four to six lines of text.
- Limit each line to forty characters.
- Use phrases rather than sentences.
- Use upper and lowercase type.
- Use a simple typeface.
- Use bullets or Arabic numerals for listing.
- Allow the same amount of space at the top of each visual.
- Use color, boldface or large-sized type for emphasis.

Graphic Visuals

Studies have shown that people assimilate ideas in visual form more quickly than they process the same information in words. Therefore graphic visuals are useful for emphasizing important relationships. To create effective graphics, you'll need to select the most appropriate chart form, follow the rules of good design, and use headings to reinforce your message.

Select the most appropriate form. Because most management presentations involve numberical data, line, bar, and pie charts are the most frequently used graphic forms, although diagrams, maps, and photographs are also valuable. Tables are appropriate only when the audience must have exact numbers. By choosing the form that best fits the point you are making, you increase the likelihood that your view will be accepted as well as understood.

Line charts show change over time of one or several variables (see Exhibit 5.4).

Bar charts, whether vertical or horizontal, are useful in showing the relationship between two or more variables at one time or at several points in time (see Exhibit 5.5). Although line and bar charts are frequently used for similar purposes, the line chart is more effective in depicting change over time. The bar chart can either highlight differences between distinct time periods or compare components of a whole at different times (see Exhibit 5.6).

Exhibit 5.4
LINE CHARTS SHOW CHANGES OVER TIME.

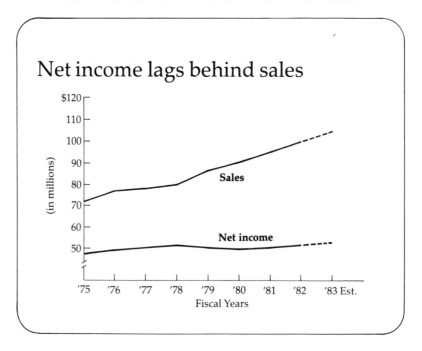

Exhibit 5.5
BAR CHARTS SHOW RELATIONSHIPS AT DISCRETE TIMES.

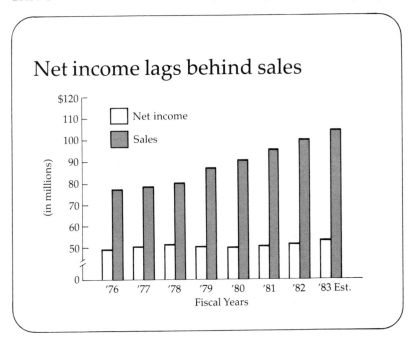

Net income lags behind sales

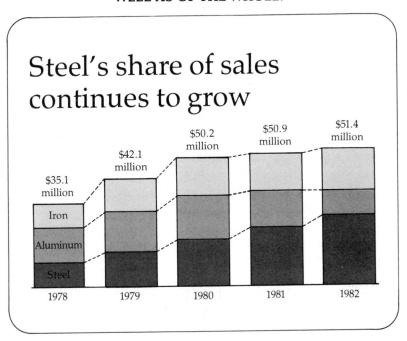

Steel's share of sales
continues to grow

Exhibit 5.7A
PIE CHARTS SHOW THE RELATIONSHIP OF THE PARTS OF A WHOLE AT A DISCRETE TIME.

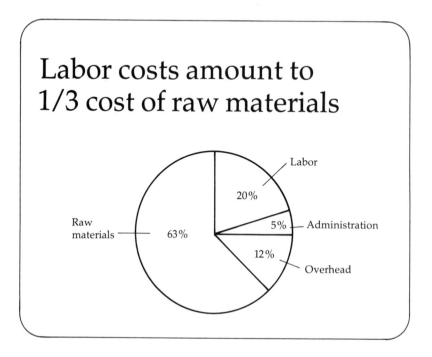

Labor costs amount to
1/3 cost of raw materials

Pie charts show the relationship among the parts of a unit at a given moment. Although pie charts are round (as in Exhibit 5.7A), other shapes can also be used to show parts of the whole (see Exhibit 5.7B). Some chartmakers believe that the most important information should be in the section beginning at 12 o'clock and extending clockwise. Others contend that people read from left to right and the most important section should be to the left of 12 o'clock. We believe the decision should be based on what looks best given the amount of data to be presented.

Diagrams, such as organization charts (Exhibit 5.8) and process charts or flow charts (Exhibit 5.9) help the audience visualize relationships and processes.

Maps focus attention on one or several locations and indicate spatial relations and distances (see Exhibit 5.10).

Drawings show the details of a design or, as cartoons, make a point with humor.

Exhibit 5.7B

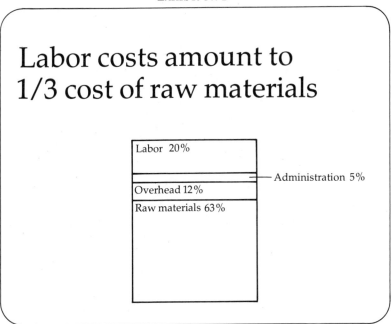

Exhibit 5.8
**DIAGRAMS SHOW THE RELATIONSHIP AMONG PARTS OF A
STRUCTURE OR UNIT.**

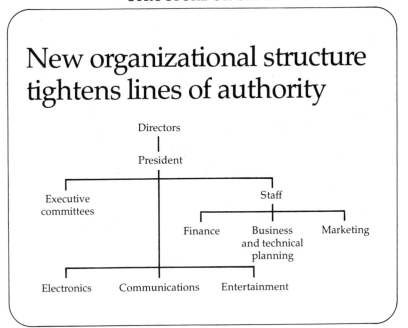

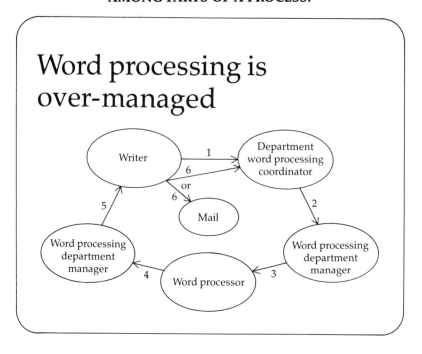

Word processing is over-managed

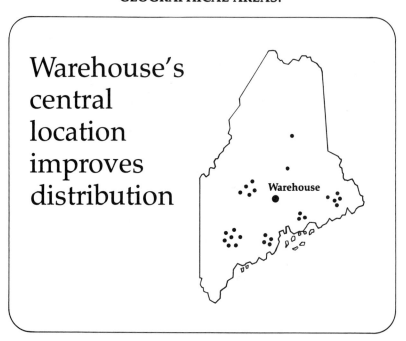

Warehouse's central location improves distribution

Photographs reproduce exact detail.

Tables provide data in a precise form. Because of their complexity, tables are rarely useful as presentation visuals. Neophyte presenters often copy a full-page table from a written document for use as an overhead or slide. Such tables, however, are inappropriate for presentations, in which the audience is expected to catch the visual message quickly. In addition, anyone beyond the first row usually cannot see long columns of numbers. If you must present all the numbers, limit them to three or four columns and three rows, or use handouts.

Guidelines for Selecting Chart Forms

Graphic Form	Function
Line chart	Change in variables over time
Bar chart	Comparison of variables at one time or several points in time
Divided bar chart	Comparison of variables and their components at fixed times
Pie chart	Relationship of components to each other or to the whole
Diagram	Parts of a process, structure, or unit
Map	Relationship of geographical locations

Follow the rules of good design. Presentation visuals are intended to be snapshots of your data, not detailed blueprints. Once you have selected an appropriate form for your chart, include only the data needed to get your message across. If you want the audience to focus on declining sales, for instance, leave out earnings and

Exhibit 5.11
**CHARTS SHOULD INCLUDE ONLY THE DATA NEEDED TO
SUPPORT THE POINT THE PRESENTER IS MAKING
VERBALLY. THE HEADING SHOULD REINFORCE THE
SPOKEN MESSAGE.**

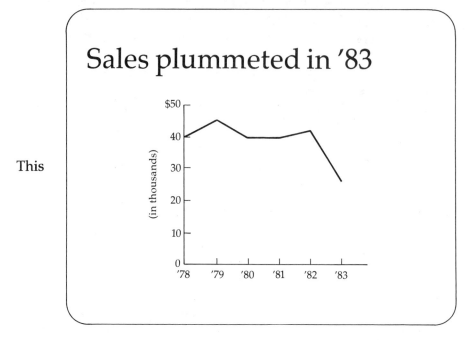

This

dividends (see Exhibit 5.11). If you're concerned that two-thirds of
corporate earnings went to pay the energy bill, a pie chart
showing all the other expenditures in detail will detract from your
message (see Exhibit 5.12).

Remember that your goal is to be simple and direct. Clearly label
any axes, data lines, or spaces, unless the subject is obvious, but
eliminate anything that does not reinforce your message, such as
grid lines (Exhibit 5.13), and keep axis lines thinner and lighter
than data lines. In bar charts, be certain the bars are wider than
the spaces between them (see Exhibit 5.14).

Don't exaggerate the data points (see Exhibit 5.15) or use more
tick marks and numbers than necessary. Too many numbers on the
axes clutter your visual (see Exhibit 5.16) and you can eliminate
digits as long as you indicate the scale on each axis. An important
value is more likely to be remembered if you note the amount on
the data line (see Exhibit 5.17) than if you try for precision by
dividing the axis into numerous subdivisions. In your attempts to

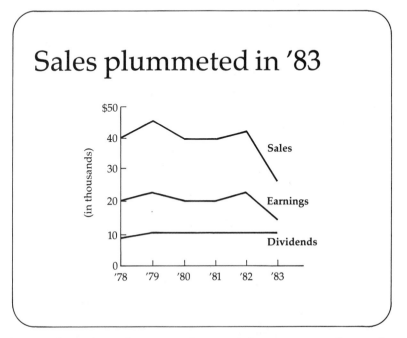

Not Thi

produce a clear chart, however, be careful not to smooth out data lines. Doing so can be misleading, and, if the audience is alert, people may suspect that you are hiding something (see Exhibit 5.18).

You can experiment with different graphic forms to find the one that is most persuasive. If you have access to a computer that accepts a graphics software package, try out a variety of configurations to determine the one most effective for your visual. For example, in Exhibits 5.19A through C, the same data appear in several formats. Although computer output may be usable in an informal presentation, many software packages do not follow all the principles of effective design, as the exhibits show. Therefore, computer graphics may not be sufficiently refined for a formal presentation. Plotters do produce acceptable graphics (Exhibit 5.19C was produced on a plotter) and further improvements in technology will make computer graphics more useful.

Color, when used in moderation, is an effective way to focus the audience's attention. You may shade part of a graph, highlight a

This

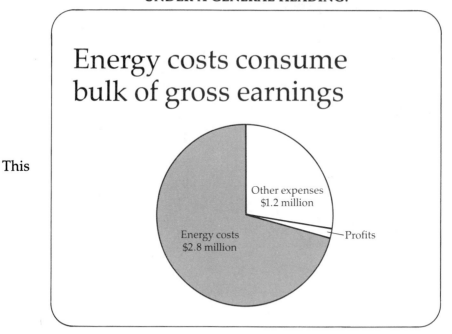

Exhibit 5.13
LINES THAT FOCUS ATTENTION ON THE CHART RATHER
THAN ON THE DATA SHOULD BE ELIMINATED.

This

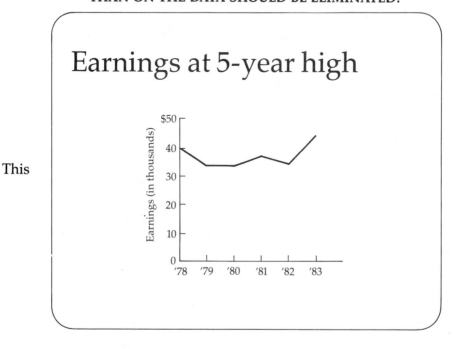

Energy costs consume bulk of gross earnings

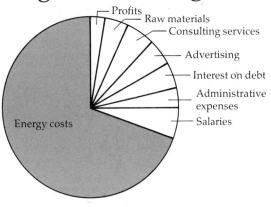

Not This

Earnings at 5-year high

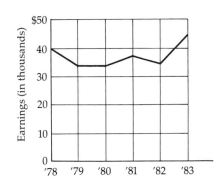

Not This

This

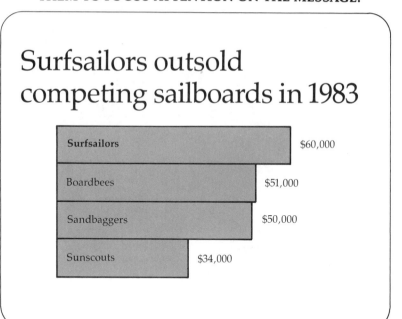

Surfsailors outsold competing sailboards in 1983

Surfsailors	$60,000
Boardbees	$51,000
Sandbaggers	$50,000
Sunscouts	$34,000

This

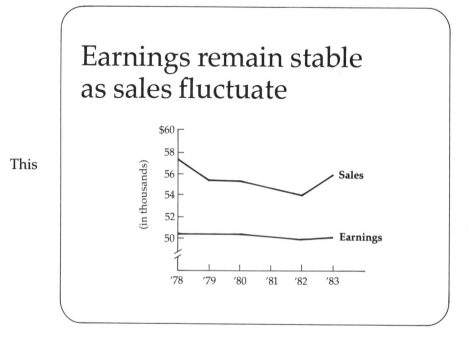

Earnings remain stable as sales fluctuate

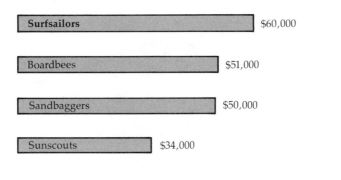

Not This

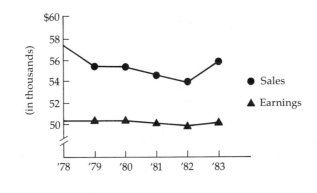

Not This

Exhibit 5.16
UNNECESSARY NUMBERS AND TICK LINES DETRACT FROM THE MESSAGE.

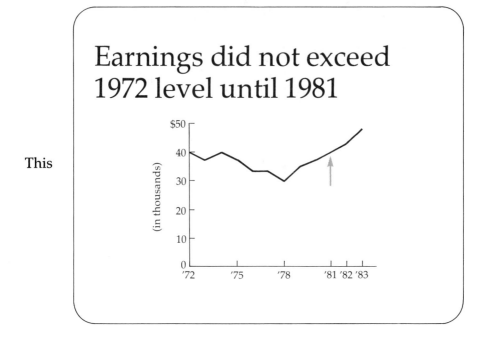

This

number, or use a colored arrow to point to details that specifically support your argument (see Exhibit 5.17). In using color, it is important to be consistent so the audience won't become confused. Remember these points when choosing colors for your visual:

- Use moderation
- Use the brightest colors to attract attention to your main point; use red sparingly.
- Use contrasting colors to suggest contrasting concepts or a major change.
- Use two shades of the same color to suggest a minor change.

Use headings to reinforce your message. A good heading makes the point of your visual explicit. If a member of the audience has been distracted while you were speaking, he or she can still see what is significant by looking at the heading. Even an attentive listener appreciates the reinforcement. The most useful heading contains a noun and a verb and tells the audience what is important. In Exhibit 5.16, for example, the heading "Earnings did not exceed 1972 levels until 1981" makes the precise point the presenter wants the audience to remember. If, on the other hand, the

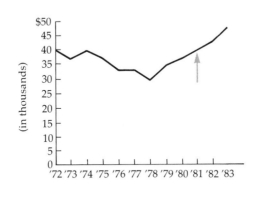

Not This

Exhibit 5.17
USE COLOR, ARROWS, AND TITLES TO FOCUS ATTENTION
ON THE POINT YOU WANT TO EMPHASIZE.

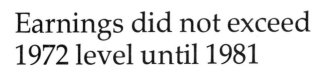

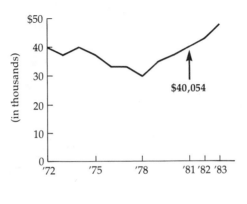

Exhibit 5.18
SMOOTHING DATA LINES MAY DISTORT THE MESSAGE.

This

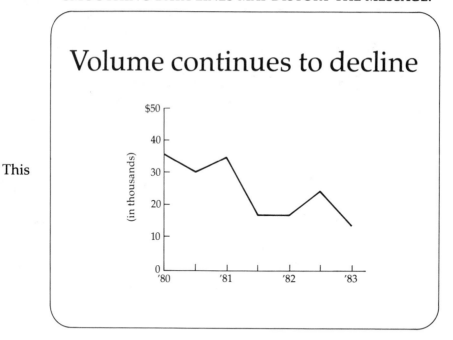

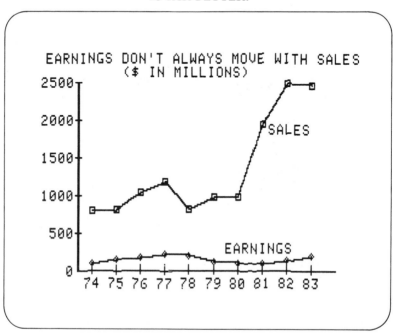

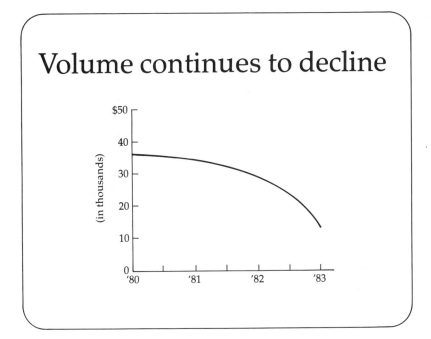

Not This

Exhibit 5.19B

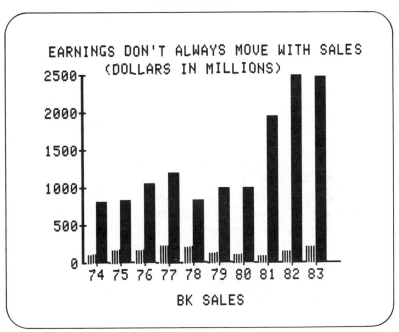

Exhibit 5.19C

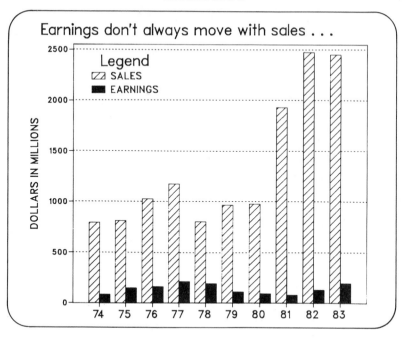

heading had been "Earnings: 1972–83," people in the audience would have been left to draw their own conclusions, and they might have come up with something the presenter didn't intend to emphasize, like "Earnings rose 20% in 1982." They might also have given up trying to decipher the meaning and missed getting any information at all. To be most effective, a good heading should have an active verb. The heading "Decline of sales traditional during second quarter," for instance, does not carry the same momentum as the heading "Sales traditionally decline during second quarter."

The design of the heading is also important. Headings should always be above the chart since we in Western cultures read from the top down; and as a rule of thumb the type should be twice as large as than any other type on the graphic. Text identifying the mechanical portions of the visual should be light while text identifying the data lines, bars, or parts in the graphic representation can be boldface. Again, for reasons of simplicity, all lettering on a visual should be of the same typeface.

These are general rules of design. In addition, there are specific guides for making and using each kind of visual aid.

Guidelines for Designing Graphic Visuals

- Limit data on a visual to what is absolutely necessary.
- Label axes, data lines, and chart areas when necessary for understanding.
- Keep chart lines thinner and lighter than data lines, omit grid lines, and don't smooth data lines.
- Use as few tick marks and numbers as possible and use rounded numbers.
- Make the spaces between bars narrower than the bars themselves.
- Don't exaggerate data points.
- Use color to highlight your message.
- Use headings to reinforce your point.

Making and Using Overheads

Overheads are more frequently used in management presentations than are flipcharts or slides because they can be easily and inexpensively produced on a standard office copier. Overheads are versatile. They can be used in both formal and informal settings, and, unlike slides, they usually can be viewed without dimming the lights of the room.

Designing Overheads

Because overheads can be easily copied from printed material, some presenters try to cut corners by simply reproducing graphics from written reports. It doesn't work. The type may be too small, there may be excessive detail, and people in an audience can rarely read the material in one of these visuals during the time it is on the screen unless you dramatically slow your pace. For presentations, you must produce special visuals.

In designing a visual and selecting type size and colors, keep in mind your purpose and the qualities and limitations of the medium. Unless the data you must convey demand a different design, take advantage of the natural, horizontal form of the overhead. Work within a 7½ × 9½-inch space centered on an

8½ × 11-inch page. Anything outside these borders will not be visible on the screen.

Because the image is enlarged on the screen, any irregularities are instantly apparent to the audience, so you want to be certain your lines are straight and your letters aligned. Working on paper with light blue grid lines will help you—the blue lines will not reproduce. For a formal presentation, you may want to have the original for the overhead typeset. An alternative, which is less costly if you make many presentations, is to use a machine that prints letter strips in various sizes and fonts. Sheets of letters are also available, but setting text letter by letter is very time-consuming. If you use a typewriter, as many people do, use only type designed for speeches or headings, preferably in boldface. The most commonly used and readily available font for typing overheads is called "Orator." The size is good but, unfortunately, the face has no lowercase letters. If, by luck, you have someone on your staff who is skilled in calligraphy, take advantage of that skill. Neat, hand-lettered visuals are generally more attractive than typewritten ones (see Exhibit 5.20).

Exhibit 5.20
HAND-LETTERED VISUALS CAN BE AS ATTRACTIVE AS
PRINTED ONES.

WE RECOMMEND THAT YOU...

- SELL MAGNET WIRE AND CABLE-CONNECTOR PRODUCT LINES.

- MANAGE COMPANY AS RISK-BALANCED PORTFOLIO OF PRODUCTS.

- RESTRUCTURE COMPANY INTO THREE DIVISIONS.

Exhibit 5.21
OVERLAYS SHOULD BE SECURELY ATTACHED TO THE OVERHEAD FRAME.

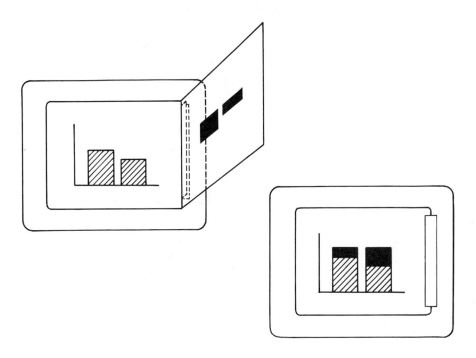

Although there are many mathematical equations that can help you determine appropriate letter size, the simplest way to check an overhead is to stand ten feet away from it. If you can read it with the naked eye, your viewers will be able to read it when it's projected.

Light lettering on a dark background, preferably blue, is easier on the viewer's eyes than dark type on a clear transparency. Special office copiers are available that can produce these negative images. However, if you don't have such a copier, don't try to add variety by using transparencies in several different colors with black type. These confuse and distract the audience. Clear transparencies are the most readily available and are always acceptable.

We urge you to control any impulse to use one overhead with multiple overlays. If you want to use an overlay for emphasis, use only one (see Exhibit 5.21). We once watched a presenter totally befuddle his audience in an attempt to uncover a decision tree, part by part. He had so many pieces of paper taped to the transparency that it became a game of hide-and-seek. If you want to uncover a chart piece-by-piece, use several transparencies in sequence. It may be less dramatic, but it is infinitely less risky.

When your overheads are completed, secure them in cardboard frames with transparent tape. Not only do the frames block out extraneous light, but, without them, transparencies often stick together or slither away and fall to the floor. As a last step, number the top right corner of each transparency so you can find your place in case one falls out of sequence.

Guidelines for Making Overheads

- Work within a horizontal 7½ × 9½-inch space.
- Work on graph paper with light blue grids.
- Check overheads for readability of type size.
- Use the most professional lettering available.
- Use light lettering on a dark transparency if possible.
- Use transparencies of one color only.
- Use no more than one overlay on any overhead.
- Secure transparencies to cardboard frames.
- Number each transparency.

Using Overheads

Using overheads professionally is important. This means your equipment must be in good working order, and you must know how to use it. Before anyone arrives, turn the projector on and off, check the focus, and insure that you have an extra bulb. (Know how to change the bulb if it goes out in the middle of your presentation.)

During the presentation, be certain that the visual on the screen amplifies the point you are making. If you finish the topic, and do not have a visual for your next point, turn the projector off. A glowing, empty screen is a dreadful distraction, and a covered transparency with light leaking around the edges is almost as bad.

Furthermore, by turning the projector off, you signal members of the audience to return their attention to you. (And should you walk between the projector and the screen, you will save yourself the embarrassment of suddenly having your mid-section appear in the spotlight.)

Where you position yourself throughout the presentation is important so that you don't block anyone's view. After you project a transparency, move far to one side and give everyone a chance to absorb the message. It helps to go through a dry run in the room you will be using. Ask a friend to check the best places for you to stand. When you are near the screen and want to point to something, don't turn your back to the audience. Instead, point with the hand nearest the screen or use a pointer if the screen is large (see Exhibit 5.22). If you do not have a pointer and you need one urgently, tightly roll up a large piece of paper on the diagonal and tape it closed. A pointer can be very useful so long as you remem-

Exhibit 5.22
ALWAYS POSITION YOURSELF SO YOU CAN POINT TO THE SCREEN WITHOUT TURNING YOUR BACK TOWARD THE AUDIENCE.

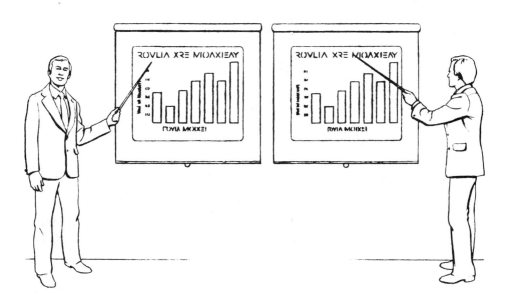

ber that it is not a toy. Beating it on the screen or waving it in circles as you talk is unprofessional and distracting.

If you are near the projector, point on the transparency with a pencil (your finger would look enormous) or, using a pen designed for the purpose, circle the concept you want to emphasize. Some presenters add information to a transparency while its image is on the screen. Although writing on the transparency during the presentation adds a sense of action to your talk, it requires good handwriting and self-assurance. It is difficult to write on a transparency without having your hand shake (the projector will magnify the movement many times over) and without moving the transparency. If you do write on the transparency, always stand to one side of the machine as you write, and then move away so everyone in the audience can read what you have written.

Guidelines for Using Overheads

- Be certain you are familiar with the operation of the projector.
- Turn the projector off whenever you are not discussing the points shown on a transparency.
- Be certain neither you nor the projector blocks anyone's view.
- Don't turn your back to the audience.
- Use a pencil rather than your finger to note a detail on the transparency.
- Write on a transparency only if you are very confident.

Making and Using Flipcharts

Flipcharts (and the easels that hold them) come in several sizes, from small table-top versions to large 30 × 40-inch charts. The size you choose depends on readability, the size of the audience, and your own height. A table-top chart may be appropriate if you are sitting around a small table with no more than four people. If you are standing, your own height becomes a factor. A large person looks Gulliver-like manipulating a small chart, and a small person who has to jump up to turn the pages of a giant flipchart may get a nervous laugh but not much empathy.

Designing Flipcharts

In making flipcharts, keep in mind the size and shape of the chart and the distance between the chart and members of the audience. Because most flipcharts are made to stand in a vertical position, your visual should be drawn on the vertical. The letters must be large enough and dark enough for every member of the audience to see. (Usually only the darkest colors and the widest felt-tip pens will work.) Test for readability by setting your chart up in a room equivalent to the one you'll be using. By standing in the most distant spot someone can reasonably be expected to sit, you can see for yourself whether every word of text and every line is readable. As a rule of thumb, letters must be 1½ inches high to be visible 25 feet away.

As you create the visuals for a flipchart presentation, leave several blank pages between visuals. That way, if you make a mistake you can draw another without worrying about re-ordering the pages. Just before you give the presentation, leave one blank sheet between every two visuals and remove the rest. The blank sheet assures that the colors from the charts underneath won't show through, and turning to it is the equivalent of turning off the overhead projector—it alerts the audience to return its attention to you.

Guidelines for Making Flipcharts

- Choose a chart size that is appropriate for the design, your height, and the size of the audience.
- Draw your art to fit the vertical shape of the chart.
- Make lettering dark enough and large enough to be read by everyone in the audience.
- While you're preparing the charts, leave several blank pages between each one to allow for corrections or additions.
- For your final presentation, remove all but one blank page before each visual.

Using Flipcharts

Flipcharts are easy to use because they require no electrical equipment. Before your presentation, be sure the easel is securely anchored on the floor, and the flipchart is firmly attached to the easel. If you are using an adjustable floor stand, set the height so you can comfortably grasp the page in the middle and flip it over the pad (see Exhibit 5.23). Also, be sure the chart braces are fixed in advance to avoid having your charts slide to the floor as you speak.

Before the audience arrives, open the chart to the first blank page. As you proceed from one visual to the next during the presentation, grasp and flip over the completed visual and the blank page following. Flip the visual with the hand nearest the flipchart as you face the audience. (If you are not ambidextrous, stand on the side most convenient for you.) If you do not have a visual for

Exhibit 5.23
TO FLIP A CHART, GRAB THE PAGE AT THE MIDDLE WITH THE HAND NEAREST THE CHART AS YOU FACE THE AUDIENCE.

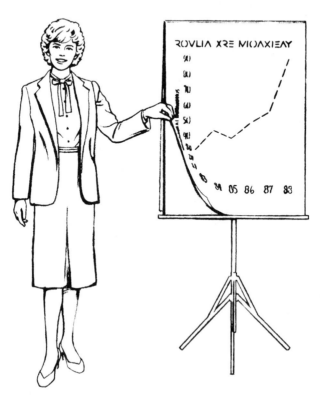

the next section of your presentation, flip to the blank page and move to another part of the room. As in any presentation, be certain to face the audience at all times. We don't recommend writing your notes in light pencil on the flipchart because we've seen presenters lose their place while they were trying to decipher their notes.

Occasionally, for external presentations, presenters use professionally made boards the size of flipchart visuals. These are tricky to use (for one thing, it's hard to find a place for the discarded boards), bulky to transport, and usually require the help of an assistant (which is distracting). These boards require such an investment of time and money that some corporations design presentations in order to reuse them. Although many consulting firms find them useful, they may be impractical for the usual internal presentation.

Guidelines for Using Flipcharts

- Securely attach the flipchart to the easel.
- Adjust the easel height before the presentation.
- Leave a blank page on top at the beginning of your presentation and turn to a blank page when there is no relevant visual.
- Grasp the visual in the middle to flip it.
- Always face your audience.

Making and Using Slides

Audiences expect slide presentations to be highly professional. A slide presentation cannot be put together at the last minute and, unless you are a crack photographer and know a good deal about graphic design, requires professional assistance. For these reasons alone, slide presentations are usually limited to major events, such as annual meetings or public relations presentations. If you are thinking about a slide presentation, consider the relationship you want with your audience. For the most part, management presentations involve a give-and-take between the presenter and the audience. Slide presentations, by their nature, discourage interruptions. In most settings, the presenter may not see the audience because the lights are dim. Under these conditions, it is impossible to tell whether people are following your argument or whether you need to adjust to a change in mood. If someone does manage to interrupt with a question, you are at a further disadvantage. You must always answer a question when it is asked; otherwise, the questioner will continue to concentrate on the unanswered question instead of on your argument. If you need a visual to respond, you will have to move rapidly through a number of slides. No matter how fast you flip through them, the audience will invariably strain to see each one. Once you have responded, you may find that locating your place again is painful and time-consuming. If you don't need a visual to support your answer, you are caught between turning off the machine and causing everyone to blink from the light change or leaving the machine on and suffering the distraction as you speak.

The advantage of using slides is the ease with which they can be transported. The development of new photographic equipment will make it increasingly easy to make slides, and desk-top projection equipment will make it easy to show slides—thus eliminating two of the traditional disadvantages of the medium.

Designing Slides

If the size of the group or the need for photographic evidence demands a slide presentation, prepare your material carefully. Pacing is all important because you cannot turn the projector on and off to insert ideas for which there is no visual support. Therefore, you'll need a slide for each part of your presentation, including the transitions.

When you work with slides, allow plenty of time for artistic and mechanical failures. They are certain to occur. When you are designing a slide, work in an area with the 2-to-3 ratio of a slide (6 × 9 inches, for example) to be sure the proportions of the visual are appropriate. If you are photographing typed material, be sure it is in boldface and in a size used for speeches or headings. Then, in general, follow the guidelines for making overheads.

Guidelines for Designing Slides

- Design visuals for continuous viewing.
- Allow sufficient production time.
- Design all visuals based on the 2-to-3 ratio of a slide.
- Photograph boldface, simple, large-sized type.
- Follow the guidelines for making overheads.

Using Slides

Since an effective slide presentation requires careful orchestration, conscientious planning and rehearsing are important. Check to be sure all the slides in the carousel or tray are right side up and in the correct order. You should always use your slides as your notes; a lectern light is disconcerting to the audience. Also, unless the slide projector has a remote control, it is critical to rehearse several times with the projectionist before the presentation. If you have to say, "Next slide, please," you'll interrupt the flow of thought for both yourself and the audience.

Use a pointer to focus the audience's attention. Some presenters use a light pointer, which allows them to point with a ray of light to a spot on the screen. However, the novelty of this tool may cause your audience to focus on the pointer more than on the point, and your dependence on yet another battery and bulb increases the chances of something going wrong. Unless you have a very large, high screen, we suggest you use a conventional pointer.

Guidelines for Using Slides

- Check the position and order of the slides in your carousel or tray.
- Use your slides as notes.
- Rehearse with the projectionist.
- Use a conventional pointer.

Computers in Presentations

Over the next few years, computers will become an increasingly useful vehicle both for producing visuals before a presentation and for developing visuals during a presentation. Their use will expand as managers become more comfortable with computers and as easier-to-use programs are developed.

Computers can be programmed to produce a series of visuals from memory, which results in a presentation similar to one using an overhead projector. The preparation, however, is more complex, the risk of electronic failure ruining the presentation is greater, and the newness of the "toy" may divert the audience's attention. As a result, at this stage in computer development, it is preferable to use the computer to generate visuals and then to convert a hard copy of the graphic into a transparency that can be used on an overhead projector.

The opportunity to play "what if?" games with a small number of participants is probably the most attractive use for computers in presentations. A graphic display of the effect a small change in one variable can have on other variables is far more useful than an hour's discussion. In order to use the computer this way, the presenter must decide which graphic form best displays the data as well as what and how much data manipulation is valuable. Although experience can help with the first decision, the second is more difficult. Because the ability to generate data with little or no effort is seductive, presenters will have to guard against creating useless variations and playing superfluous games that do not serve the purposes of the presentation. Done effectively, however, these presentations are both exciting (because the computer enforces a sense of forward movement) and persuasive.

A Last Word

This chapter has dealt with designing and using visuals. There is one last cardinal rule: check all visuals for errors. Nothing can damage a fine presentation as quickly as a typographical error. Before you go to the next step in preparing your presentation, review all visuals carefully and ask an outsider or a disinterested co-worker to review them for errors, inconsistencies, or points of confusion. Then you can set them aside until you are ready to rehearse.

SUMMARY

- In choosing among overheads, flipcharts, and slides, consider
  —the formality of the presentation
  —the complexity of the data
  —the conventions of the industry and the organization
  —the size of the audience
  —the availability of resources
- Both text and graphic visuals should be simple and should focus attention on your message
- Select the chart form that best makes your point
- Use color to reinforce your message
- Headings provide a special opportunity to emphasize your point. They should contain a noun and an active verb and clearly state what you want the audience to remember
- During the presentation be careful *not to*
  —leave irrelevant visuals in front of the audience
  —block the audience's view of a visual
  —turn your back to the audience
- Always review visuals for typographical and conceptual errors

6

SETTING THE STAGE

With all the effort you've put into preparing the presentation, you may be tempted to let someone else take care of the staging. Although a competent aide can help with some of the details, the presenter has ultimate responsibility for:

- Briefing the audience
- Preparing the handouts
- Working out procedures
- Making room arrangements
- Managing the miscellaneous details

Briefing the Audience

Many presentations take place within the context of a meeting. As the presenter, you may be responsible for or participate in selecting the people who attend. The quality of the discussion that follows the presentation depends in large part on how carefully you select, notify, and brief those who attend.

Checking the List of Participants

Before you developed the presentation, you made a list of participants. Now is the time to check that list to insure that no one important has been omitted and that only those who have a stake in the outcome remain on the list. In all too many organizations, the invitation list for a presentation simply duplicates the general distribution list for company memoranda. The danger in this lack of selectivity is that some people attend merely because they don't want to "miss out on" something. Then they disrupt the presentation with irrelevant questions or self-serving statements. If indiscriminate invitations are the norm in your company and you want to cut back the list to a sensible level, make sure you talk to those you intend to exclude well in advance of the presentation. If you do, you'll find many who will be happy to miss another meeting and be quite satisfied with a phone call or memo to keep them informed.

Notifying Participants

When possible, the presentation notification should come from the most senior person in the organization who will attend the meeting. That notification should be in writing and should clearly state the purpose of the presentation. Naturally, participants should be notified well in advance. If most of those invited do not know you personally, a comment noting your expertise on the presentation topic should be included. A brief statement like the one on the next page is sufficient.

Alert Participants to Advance Work

Although conscientious managers prepare for any meeting they attend, as the presenter, it's your responsibility to tell participants how much advance work you expect them to do. The level of preparation depends on their backgrounds, the norms of the

```
To:   Mike Wylie

From: Jill Howard

Re:   October 25th presentation detailing
      quality circle recommendations
     On October 25th, Forrest Ross will make a 45-
minute presentation to all senior officers
detailing the recommendation of our internal
consultants that we introduce quality circles in
our Midwest region plants. Mr. Ross, who has been
with Gotham Motors for 15 years, spent six months
studying the program at the Iliad Motor's San
Antonio plant before heading the consulting team
for this project.
```

organization, the purpose of the presentation, and the complexity of the subject.   .

Consider briefing all those who have not participated in earlier discussions of the topic, either by conferring with them individually or by sending them notes of the discussions. These preliminaries insure that you won't have to explain the basics during the presentation itself.

In some organizations, the presenter circulates a quantity of material for participants to read before the meeting. In other organizations, no one ever receives more advance information than can be absorbed on the subway between Grand Central Station and Wall Street (twenty minutes on a good day). There is little point in going against the norms of the organization in this case because you risk dividing the group. For instance, people who did their homework will be angry if you rehash familiar details; those who did not read the information you sent out will be lost if you don't repeat.

When substantial advance work is the norm, problem-solving meetings are frequently preceded by the distribution of a written evaluation of the alternatives. The presentation itself is then used to fill in details and answer questions. If the subject is very complex and those attending have technical expertise in the field, you may speed up the actual presentation by distributing difficult statistical data in advance. If you do hand out material in advance, do not repeat it verbatim in the presentation. If you repeat material you've asked people to read, you are implying that they are unable to grasp your point.

Preparing Handouts

Many presenters use handouts, even though they are time-consuming to produce and often are perceived by some members of the audience as a waste of paper. Before preparing handouts, consider whether you need:

- a working handout that clarifies an essential point or issue
- a take-away handout that participants can refer to in making future decisions or in implementing a plan

Working handouts should be used only when the information is so complex that it can't be put on a flipchart, overhead, or slide. Don't be tempted to reproduce a composite ten-year income statement, however, when your audience needs only four columns of figures. The typeset report may look elegant and its sophistication may distract the audience from some unsettling points, but nothing can justify the time lost as mystified people try to absorb all the details. Include only data necessary to the discussion.

If someone else prepares your handout, be sure you understand everything on it. One presenter, who had accepted his associate's work without question, when asked to explain the significance of a column of figures to the board of directors, struggled for some minutes and finally said, "I'm not sure, but they don't add up to anything." A board member later remarked, "It wasn't a pretty sight."

Hand out material as the audience needs it rather than distributing it before the presentation. Although giving it out during the presentation interferes with your pacing, you will discourage a division between those who have read the material and those who haven't. Moreover, you will encourage the audience to pay attention to what you are saying. Otherwise, people will flip through the printed material while you are speaking.

Take-away handouts are meant as a review, and thus should remind the reader of the major points in your argument and their significance. You may be tempted to make paper copies of your overhead transparencies (frequently, after a speech or an external presentation, someone may ask you for copies of your visuals), but keep in mind that your visuals didn't stand alone; you elaborated on their meaning as you spoke. The two-fold job of visuals that also serve as handouts reminds us of a comment about an amphibious automobile: "In trying to do two things, it does neither very well." You may want to repeat words from a visual as a reminder, but the text must be expanded. (Exhibit 6.1A and B show what a text overhead looks like after it has been converted into a handout.) Before you transform charts and graphs into handouts, annotate them to show how they support your argument. (Exhibits 6.2A and B demonstrate the difference between a graphic overhead and a handout.)

If you are going to provide take-away handouts, distribute them after the discussion that follows the presentation. Your purpose is to focus attention on the presentation or discussion, not on the handout. You may want to announce before the presentation begins, however, that you will provide handouts at the end. This reassurance may give compulsive notetakers permission to concentrate on your ideas rather than on writing down every word.

Working Out Procedures

Have you ever waited to be introduced only to discover that you were expected to introduce yourself? Or, as a panel member, been embarrassed to find that the moderator was asking you to answer a question to which you had not listened? If you iron out procedural details ahead of time, you may save yourself from such gaffes. If you are the only presenter and you know the audience well, you probably don't need to worry. If, however, the presentation is formal and there are several presenters, everyone must know exactly what is going to happen.

Introductions

Because an introduction sets the tone, it is wise to rehearse, whether you are introducing yourself or someone else. In a formal setting, the person who called the meeting or arranged for the presentation will usually make the introduction. Although if you are the presenter, you may not have much influence on what is said, try to talk to this person. Suggest an appropriate introduction,

Exhibit 6.1A
A TEXT VISUAL SERVES AS A GUIDE TO THE FORM THE
SPOKEN MESSAGE IS TAKING.

Organizational structure allows:

- Neglect of key tasks

- Overdependence on key people

- Uneven work distribution

- Poor communication

- Limited staff involvement

Exhibit 6.1B
A HANDOUT MUST SUMMARIZE THE SPOKEN
MESSAGE AND PROVIDE ENOUGH INFORMATION TO
STAND ALONE AFTER THE PRESENTATION IS OVER.

Organizational structure has allowed these weaknesses to develop:

- Key tasks are not being performed: market research, long-range planning, proposal writing, development of an integrated advertising policy

- The organization is overly dependent on key people: two individuals manage all aspects of the program

- Work is unevenly distributed: several departments are overloaded, others are underutilized

- Communication among departments is poor

- The staff's involvement in the organization is artificially limited:
  Skills not immediately applicable are not being developed
  Talents are not being adequately used
  Individuals know only one area and miss interrelationships
  Tasks are cyclical, providing little real diversity

Exhibit 6.2A
A GRAPHIC VISUAL MUST BE SIMPLE.

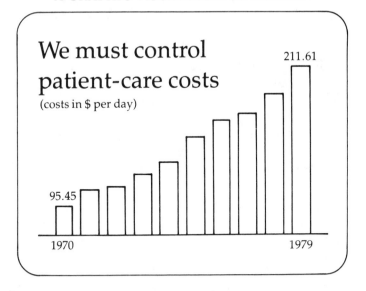

Exhibit 6.2B
A HANDOUT MUST BE EXPANDED TO EXPLAIN THE
VISUAL IMAGE.

especially if you believe your credentials need to be established, and ask that he or she state the purpose of the presentation. If several presenters are involved, introductions can become clumsy. The person who called the meeting may introduce all the presenters or only the team leader. It is important to be clear in advance which it will be. If only the leader is introduced, he or she should introduce all the team members before the presentation begins and indicate the level of each one's participation. If team members who are present will not participate in the presentation itself, their contribution to the presentation should be recognized. For example, the team leader might say, "On my right is Herbert Andersen, who prepared the computer software analysis."

Dealing with Questions

If you are the only presenter, you handle the questions. When there is a panel or when team members, who are not directly involved in the presentation, are available as experts, the individual who presents the information is expected to answer related questions. If you, as the presenter, decide to defer to someone else, repeat the question (if there is any possibility that someone has not heard it) or restate it (if you feel it needs to be clarified)— then direct it to the appropriate person. Occasionally, team members who are not directly involved in the presentation are asked to field questions as a way of including them in the discussion. We've never seen this work. Invariably, the person delegated to answer questions either turns to a presenter for elaboration (which projects confusion and lack of professionalism) or another member interrupts with additional information (which projects conflict or rivalry).

Using Visuals

Whenever possible, the presenter should manipulate the visuals. A false ethic of cooperation sometimes leads a presenter to ask another team member to assist. Not only does this practice demean the person running the equipment but the cuing also distracts the audience. If someone else must handle your visuals (either because you are using slides or heavy boards or because the room arrangement does not allow you freedom to move), only several rehearsals with your assistant and a back-up person will establish a smooth cuing system.

Making Room Arrangements

Making room arrangements involves more than finding an empty room. As you plan the presentation, arrange for an appropriate room, check the position of the audiovisual equipment, and decide on a seating layout.

We once arrived, transparencies in hand, expecting to make a presentation to an audience of 30. We had asked ahead of time for an overhead projector and screen. Much to our surprise, we discovered that 110 people had registered for the program. The room had been changed to accommodate the larger number and a tabletop easel and pad (but no felt-tipped marker) had been substituted for the projector. For the next two hours, we drew organization trees in the air—undoubtedly a waste of time for everyone. In a management setting, you are not likely to confront quite so extreme a situation because you can have more control over your location and the arrangements. However, stories of malfunctioning overheads and poorly arranged seating are legion. Careful attention to detail can mean the difference between a well-received presentation and a disaster.

The Right Room

The size of your meeting room has a psychological as well as a physical impact on the audience. Although people will crowd into a room to hear a celebrity, a group of top executives, who have to sit elbow-to-elbow in an overheated conference room and put up with a presenter who can't find a spot for the overhead, will feel insulted and will probably focus their irritation on the presenter. For management presentations, the room should be large enough to accommodate everyone comfortably but small enough to provide a sense of community. If a room of appropriate size is not available, choose a room that is slightly too small rather than too large. Six people meeting at one end of a cavernous hall are likely to feel uneasy, like members of a primitive tribe huddling around a campfire.

Location of Visual Aid Equipment

In some rooms, the screens are permanently installed and therefore dictate the seating arrangement. As a result, it is important to think about the location of your visual aid equipment before you settle on a seating arrangement. Ideally, if you are using overheads or slides, place the screen off center and angled slightly in relation to the audience. (Exhibits 6.3 through 6.6 show the placement of screens and equipment for various seating arrangements.) With the screen off center, you can stand in front of the audience without blocking anyone's view of the visual. If possible, position the

CONFERENCE TABLE SEATING ARRANGEMENTS

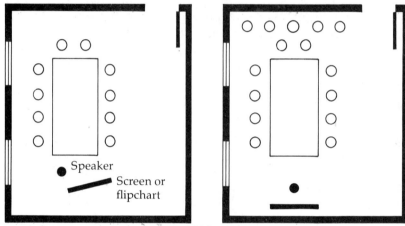

Exhibit 6.3
A conference table provides most appropriate setting for a presentation followed by a discussion. In the arrangement on the right, the speaker is blocking the screen, and those not seated at the table are effectively excluded.

U-SHAPED SEATING ARRANGEMENTS

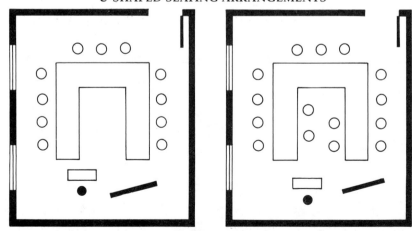

Exhibit 6.4
A U-shaped arrangement accommodates more people than a conference table; however, participants should never be seated in the center of a U-shaped arrangement where they cannot see others without turning.

screen so it is above the level of people's heads and slant it toward the audience to create a perpendicular between the screen's plane and the axis of the projector beam. This perpendicular keeps the image a true square or a rectangle. (Many screens can be adjusted by moving the loop that hooks the screen to the upright that holds it.)

AUDITORIUM-STYLE SEATING ARRANGEMENTS

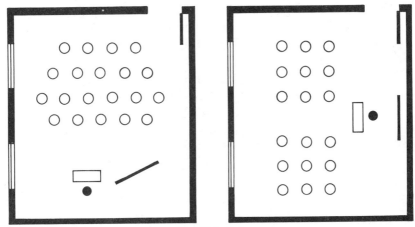

Exhibit 6.5
In this "classroom" arrangement on the left, every participant has a clear line of vision. On the right, any exit or entry will create a distraction; the center aisle creates two groups; and the presenter blocks the participants' view of the screen.

SEMICIRCULAR SEATING ARRANGEMENTS

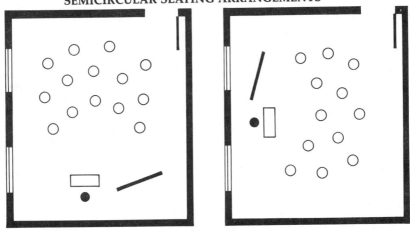

Exhibit 6.6
The semicircle is the best arrangement for a large group, but avoid the arrangement on the right where the glare from the windows (even with shades drawn) will interfere with the participants' ability to see.

Seating Arrangements

The most critical factor in arranging seating is the size of the audience. Within the limitations of room size, door and window locations and permanently installed screens, choose the seating arrangement that puts the fewest barriers between you and the audience and that permits the easiest exchange of information.

The most effective seating arrangement for a presentation that leads to a problem-solving session is around a conference table (see Exhibit 6.3). This set-up suggests to participants that "We're all in this together." It works, however, only when no one has to turn around to see the visuals and when everyone has a seat at the table. If some participants have to sit in a row against the wall, they will feel distinctly second class.

A U-shaped arrangement (see Exhibit 6.4) accommodates more poeple and facilitates discussion as long as all the participants can see each other easily. It does, however, separate the presenter from the audience.

An auditorium or classroom arrangement (see Exhibit 6.5) is often used for a large audience. This arrangement discourages participation and note-taking, and conveys the message: "I'll do the talking; you listen." The audiences for most management presentations are so small that this configuration is not appropriate, but if you must present in a large auditorium, always try to unify the group by having people move forward. If the chairs aren't fixed, eliminate the center aisle, which has a divisive effect.

A semicircle (see Exhibit 6.6) is less formal than the classroom configuration and permits better communication among members of the audience. For a large group, it may be the best arrangement.

Regardless of what seating arrangement you finally choose, some rules of thumb are:

- Make sure chairs are comfortable enough for people to sit without squirming but not so comfortable that they encourage napping. Chairs with arms and firm cushions and backs are preferable.
- Arrange seating so the audience does not face the windows. Not only is the scene outside distracting, but the audience will have to squint to see the visuals.
- Arrange seating so the door is to the rear or the side of the group. Once in a while, a participant will have to leave before you're finished. No one can exit gracefully or unobtrusively by walking in front of you.

Managing the "Odds and Ends"

The term "odds and ends" may sound casual, but presentation pros have learned, through years of experience, that attention to apparently minor details can be crucially important to the success of a presentation. Many managers develop their own checklists for such logistical elements as the location of the meeting, the person responsible for equipment, and arrangements for messages and refreshments. They also keep a list of the supplies they know they'll need. These needs will vary from presenter to presenter and from presentation to presentation, but keeping track of details with checklists will save you from last-minute phone calls and frantic scrambling. If you use the checklists below and on page 124 as models, and add to them each time you review a presentation, you will ultimately develop lists that cover any contingency you're likely to encounter.

Checklist
Presentation Logistics

Presentation Topic _____

　　　　　Date _____ Time _____

　　　　　Location _____ Contact Person _____

Presenter _____

Number of participants _____ Announcements sent (date) _____

Person responsible for setting up _____ Tel. No. _____

Seating arrangement (including number of chairs) _____

Location of restrooms _____

Location of telephones _____

Visual equipment _____

Lectern? _____ Microphone? _____ Lavalier? _____

Water/pitcher/glasses _____

Refreshments _____

　　　(Person responsible _____ Tel. No. _____)

Handout materials _____

Checklist

Supplies

visuals
extra projector bulbs
spare parts for projector
converter plug
extension cord(s)
felt-tipped pens (different colors)
masking tape
stick pins
extra eyeglasses
chalk
erasers
blank transparencies
pointer
tent cards
extra handouts
extra agendas
marking pens for transparencies
lozenges

_____

_____

In addition, you may want to put together a traveling kit of those supplies you use most frequently—ours includes tape, tacks, tent cards, markers for flipcharts, markers for overheads, spare overheads, a pointer, extra pens and pencils.

For the typical management presentation you won't need to allow for a break, although you will want to see that water is available. For a small group, a water pitcher and glasses should be on the table in front of the participants; for a large group, water should be available at the rear of the room. Any meeting that lasts more than an hour and a half demands a break. As more than one experienced presentation-goer has remarked, "The mind absorbs no more than the seat will bear." Serving coffee or caffeinated drinks as well as refreshments with sugar during the break will help keep your audience alert.

A planned break is no problem, but sudden interruptions for the delivery of emergency messages can be a nuisance. It is important that you devise some system for notifying participants unobtrusively. Again, in a small group, you can have your secretary come in and hand you a note. In that way, you can stay in charge of your pacing. In a large auditorium or hotel setting, we have found it works to arrange for someone to come to the front of the room and hold up a large placard with the person's name clearly printed. It is also possible to have someone hand a message to you so that you can decide the appropriate place to break in and say quietly: "Shirley, there's a call for you at the front desk."

SUMMARY

- Properly selecting and briefing the audience is critical to a successful presentation:
  —limit the audience to those people with a stake in the outcome
  —notify the audience well in advance
  —provide whatever information participants need to prepare for the presentation
- Working handouts provide your audience with technical data and should be distributed as they are needed during the presentation
- Take-away handouts are reminders of the discussion. They should be more complete than visuals used during the presentation and should be distributed after the presentation.
- Everyone involved should agree in advance on the procedures for introducing participants, answering questions, and using visuals
- The size of the group and the purpose of the meeting dictate the seating arrangement. The location of doors, windows, and electrical equipment influence the room arrangement.
- Every presenter should have logistics and supplies checklists

7

REHEARSING AND DELIVERING THE PRESENTATION

Once you've developed your argument and your visual support, you are ready to:
- Rehearse effectively
- Present yourself with confidence
- Deal with interruptions gracefully
- Manage the question-and-answer period
- Evaluate your presentation

Rehearsing Effectively

Chances are you weren't hired for your speaking ability. Furthermore, if your early training stressed analytical or technical skills, you may think all presenters are performing bears and, for that reason, resist joining their ranks. Your objection, in part, may be a rationalization based on lack of confidence or even resentment that you are asked to do something you weren't hired to do and don't believe you're good at. Rehearsals can help you overcome these feelings. Not everyone is born with a well-pitched, resonant voice, but, with practice everyone can develop a speaking style that makes the most of whatever he or she does have. (Clearly, if you have severe speech problems, you'll need to consult a professional in that field.) Rehearsals help you to develop a sense of timing and to master the material, both of which are vital to a smooth delivery.

If you're not used to rehearsing, speaking to an audience that doesn't exist may seem slightly silly at first. By taking the time to practice in private, however, you will find the presentation itself less nerve-racking. After all, having said it all before, you'll be able to relax, concentrate on the audience, and even have some fun. If the idea of making a presentation is extremely anxiety-provoking, you can go through your own desensitization process, similar to what psychologists recommend for phobias, as you rehearse. Start by visualizing yourself giving the presentation, and then make each successive rehearsal a closer approximation of the real thing. The idea is to familiarize yourself with what you expect from the actual situation so that your fears subside and don't get between you and making a good presentation.

Even if you are not particularly anxious about giving a presentation, rehearse three times: once alone facing a mirror; another time before a supportive but uninvolved listener; and, finally, in front of two or three friends. In this final rehearsal, try to use the room in which you'll be presenting and the equipment you will use during the presentation. Rehearsing in front of the mirror will help you modify your wording so that the presentation will flow. Ask your listeners to raise questions and comment on your style, timing, and professional tone. Because most people are timid about giving criticism, always ask them specific questions: Did they understand the main point? Did they agree with you? Could they repeat your major supporting statements?

Electronic equipment, which is easy to use and frequently available, can be very helpful during rehearsals. Using a tape recorder, for example, will make you conscious of slang expressions and annoying repetitions that creep into everyday speech. Videotaping provides even more specific feedback—your gestures and movements can be very revealing. The final rehearsal is not the time to make your first videotape, however. Although some people are pleasantly surprised when they see the way they actually appear to others, some are shocked. One man promptly shaved off his moustache when a videotape revealed how much time he spent stroking it. To avoid unpleasant surprises that may damage your self-confidence, make your first videotape either a dry run or a rehearsal for some minor talk. If your organization doesn't have the equipment, you may be able to find a course in presentations that includes an opportunity to videotape. Once you've adjusted to seeing yourself as others see you, you'll find videotaping a terrific bonus.

Timing the Presentation and Developing Your Pace

During rehearsals, work on your timing so that the presentation fits into the allotted schedule and develop a good sense of pacing so that you can control the unfolding of your argument. Some people speed up when they present (usually those who tend to treat stress as a call to action), others slow down (usually those whose response tends to be more possum-like). To get a feel for an appropriate speed, try to read half this page in two minutes (a speed of 120 words a minute is just about right, although anything up to 160 words a minute is acceptable). Although psychologists say that people tend to believe fast-talkers more than those who speak slowly and deliberately, speed has its drawbacks. One presenter, who was allotted 30 minutes for her presentation, managed to whip through it in 20 minutes. However, her audience was so befuddled that the first question was: "What did you say?" Practice can help you achieve a reasonable speed. When you read your storyboards, you checked for length. Now check again. Time the rehearsal and then subtract enough detail and supporting material so that you end five minutes before your time is up. Don't worry about filling the allotted time—no one ever condemned a presenter for ending early.

Developing a sense of pacing (that is, knowing when to slow down and when to speed up) is as essential to a well-run presentation as the ability to get from the beginning to the end in a given period of time. Because you want to give the audience the sense that the argument is unfolding deliberately and that you are progressing toward a specific goal, your pace should be fairly even. If your presentation has a great many visuals, allow approximately the same amount of time for each, but slow down for an especially important point and vary your pace when you anticipate a change in the audience's involvement. During the presentation you will want to pick up the pace if you sense your audience is growing tired. Slow down if you sense resistance or if some members of the audience don't seem to understand your message. Pacing makes the difference between an alert, interested audience and a collection of distressed people surreptitiously checking their watches.

Mastering the Material

Rehearsals allow you to feel comfortable with your presentation material. If you're rehearsing by yourself, play devil's advocate and ask yourself hard questions. Imagine what you would say if you were in the audience. Role play what the decision maker might ask. If you find yourself stumbling at any point in the presentation, it may be that you don't truly believe your argument or that you missed some flaw in the logic when you organized the presentation. Go back to your organization tree and check.

Your choice of words also reveals your mastery of the material. Rehearsals will give you the confidence to choose the strongest appropriate words. You won't be afraid to express yourself, for example, in clear, direct terms such as "Continuing on this course will be destructive" rather than "This course of action may present problems." Your speech will have much more meaning and power if you use precise, strong language. Once you've used a good, powerful word, though, don't get stuck on it. Calling three concepts "pivotal" in the same presentation dissipates the force of the word and, thus, your argument. Along the same lines, don't exaggerate. Even one exaggerated statement makes an audience suspicious, and a stream of overdone claims will undermine your whole argument.

Editing the Presentation

Just as you edit memos and reports to make sure your language is precise, use your rehearsals to eliminate weaknesses in your presentation. Although audiences are more forgiving than readers in this regard, careful editing helps you eliminate such flaws as excessive use of filler words, nonwords, jargon, acronyms, sexist language, and hidden messages.

Filler words. Some favorite fillers are "generally speaking" and "basically." You may find you have other words you slip in when you have nothing particularly earthshaking to say. "I feel that" and "I believe that" are phrases speakers commonly load onto the front of a perfectly good statement, turning it from crisp to sodden. Using "et cetera" or "and so on" suggests that you can't come up with more examples. Because any presentation involves a degree of extemporizing, you can't expect to eliminate all your filler words. By your third rehearsal, however, sheer familiarity with the presentation should have erased most of them.

Nonwords and questions. Inexperienced presenters who are terrified by silence (presumably because they fear their listeners are evaluating them) often attempt to fill every gap with "ums" or "uhs" or tentative expressions like "okay?" or "right?" You can, and should, pause to emphasize a point and to help the audience sense punctuation (that is part of pacing). As you rehearse, make yourself stop at the end of each sentence; you'll find "ums," "uhs," and "ahs" generally disappear. Keep in mind, too, that using questioning phrases reveals a subconscious need for permission to continue (because you're uncertain of your argument) or for assurance that the audience is still listening. Rehearsals make you more aware of this pattern and give you the confidence to eliminate such tentative and unconvincing phrases.

Jargon and acronyms. Jargon and acronyms are permissible only if everyone in the room understands them—and even then should be avoided. Jargon (the special language of your profession or business), in particular, should not be used in any external presentation. As a presenter, you have an obligation to deliver a fresh proposal—jargon kills that freshness. It can also date you. In his column in the *New York Times* (September 19, 1982), William Safire noted that the use of "impact" and "interface" as verbs, once popular in business circles, was dying out. Using terms like these, although not devastating to your argument, will not advance your cause as much as good, precise English. Furthermore, if your audience includes language purists, such terms will have the same effect as chalk squeaking on a blackboard. Be especially cautious about bringing in fancy words like "exogenous." Even when such words are part of your organization's written vocabulary, they are jarring to listeners.

Sexist language and hidden messages. By now everyone can accept the fact that most women work outside the home and many women are managers. It shouldn't be cause for comment, much less sexual innuendo. In fact, sexist comments may put the presenter in a very embarrassing spot and damage rapport with the audience. For example, one man referred to a colleague's all-women department as "Joe's harem." Joe was embarrassed. His subordinates were angry. Along the same lines, make sure that your examples of executives include females as well as males and that occupational categories are updated from businessman to business executive, from foreman to supervisor, and from sales-man to salesperson. It is actually easier in speaking than in writing substitute "he and she" for the generic use of "he" because the structure of spoken speech is much looser.

Sometimes the words you use say more than you want. Con-sider the consultant who alienated his potential client with an off-hand reference to the "cumbersome" survey technique he was actually trying to sell, or the army officer who spoke on "Tech-niques for *Making* Your Subordinates Participate in Decisions." Ask someone to tell you when you're rehearsing if he or she picks up hidden or double messages in the words you use.

You'll have mastered the presentation when your pace is correct, your sentences are precise and clearly delineated, your voice sounds confident (neither too loud nor too soft), and you can han-dle your visuals gracefully. Because someone engaged in present-ing is usually more energetic than someone running through a rehearsal, you can expect your presentation to be even better than your final rehearsal.

Delivering Your Presentation

Your argument is tight, and you know exactly what you want to say. Your rehearsals have made you comfortable with the material. Now you are ready to follow through with a strong delivery by taking these steps:
- Alleviate nervousness.
- Use nonverbal cues.
- Establish rapport.
- Use notes effectively.
- Speak clearly.

Alleviating Nervousness

A slight nervousness is normal for any management presenter, especially the first few times. Eventually, however, many presenters overcome the jitters (except, perhaps, for mild excitement) and allow themselves to enjoy making a presentation. Their secret is not necessarily the confidence that comes from experience, although that helps, but a change in attitude: They have learned to shift their focus from themselves to the audience.

Nervousness has two sources. One is the constant stream of internal negative comments that nags the speaker when he or she begins to think about the presentation ("I wonder how I'll come across this time?" "Last time I made a presentation, I was sure everyone was laughing at me when I had so much trouble with the projector."). The other source of tension comes from hyperresponsibility. The presenter feels that he or she alone is responsible for the reactions and well-being of everyone in the audience.

The first kind of nervousness tends to evaporate when you reprogram your thought process. If you have a logical argument and you're prepared, you can stop worrying about flaws in your reasoning and technical problems. Instead, you can focus on convincing the audience that your position is correct. Think about it this way: You believe in what you're saying. You're prepared. In fact, for this presentation, you're the only person who is so well prepared. Your audience needs to know what you have to say. With these thoughts in mind, you can proceed to change the words you say to yourself from negative messages to more positive ones. List your concerns on a sheet of paper before the presentation. Then, for every negative message, substitute a positive one. For instance, if your negative message is, "I'm a nervous wreck," write, "I can channel this nervous energy into the presentation and give a more enthusiastic performance." This effort may take numerous repetitions, but eventually it works.

The second kind of nervousness (taking responsibility for everyone in the room) can also be fought. Come to terms with the fact that everyone in the room will not necessarily accept your ideas. It's not your job to please everyone. Your job is to get your message across in clearly understandable terms to the people who must have the information. Concentrate on the decision maker and on those who respond positively to you. Forget the others.

Because it is hard to counteract nervousness if you do not feel in control of the situation, take time before the presentation begins to put yourself in control:

- Allow plenty of time to check out the room and the equipment.
- Start on time. Unless the decision maker in your audience is delayed, don't wait for laggards. Delaying will make you and your audience fidgety.

- Greet people as they come in. Chat casually with people you know until it's time to start.
- Eliminate any physical barriers that stand between the audience and you. If you're behind a table or lectern, move away from it. Don't cling to the lectern or overhead projector.

Using Nonverbal Cues

You're confident. You've rehearsed. You've got a powerful, logical argument. You're ready now to take on the task of presenting your points in such a way that you do not distract from your argument. In management presentations, the drama should be in the content, not in the person. Once you're aware of the way people react to you, you can control the way you present yourself.

Leave the appropriate distance between you and the audience. Although a public speaker may be 12 to 15 feet from the first row of listeners without being viewed as aloof and impersonal, a management presenter, who generally deals with far fewer people, should be no more than 4 to 5 feet away. If you're any farther away, the listeners may regard you as either stuffy or fearful. If you're any closer, people will become uncomfortable. When you're speaking to a group with whom you have had little or no personal or professional relationship, start speaking from a position farther away and move in slightly as the presentation progresses and as you establish rapport. But don't get too close. A tall presenter, for example, who approaches within inches of his listeners and leans forward, is expressing dominance more than friendliness. To judge whether you tend to invade others' personal space, recall whether people ever inched away from you when you were engaged in informal conversations. Physical distance rules vary from one culture to another. Arabs want to be within inches of each other when they speak, whereas the Japanese expect even more distance than Americans. When you're in another country, the best way to learn the appropriate distance to put between yourself and the audience is to observe native speakers of approximately your status.

Stand erect. Good posture gives the impression of authority. You can correct bad posture habits without difficulty by standing against a wall and pressing your spine flat against it. Unless you have abnormal curvature of the spine or other physical problems, constant repetition of this exercise will bring results. While you're making your presentation, make a conscious effort not to fold your arms. Folded arms seem to encourage slouching. There is a difference between good posture and stiffness, however. If you march briskly to the front of the room and do not move for the rest of the presentation, you signal rigidity more than authority.

Consider your appearance. Psychologists have found that attractive people are more persuasive than unattractive people. They are not referring to a model's appearance. Anyone can cultivate attractiveness through good grooming and clean, neat, professional dress. A presentation is not the place to "make a statement" with your clothes—flashy clothes divert attention from your argument. The standard business dress remains dark suits and white or blue shirts for men and conservative suits or dresses for women. In some corporations, even mild deviations from this standard, if tolerated at all, are considered the prerogative of only the very mighty. Although standards in nontraditional organizations may be more lenient, in general, it is safer to stay on the side of conservatism. Anything too far from the norm will cause the audience to fix on the distracting feature rather than your argument. We know one presenter, for example, who—forced to wear tennis shoes because of a foot problem—dyed them black to keep them unobtrusive.

Finally, even in an informal meeting, smoking makes you look nervous and is far less acceptable than it once was. And chewing gum is out. Both indicate nervousness and a lack of consideration for others.

Move about and use gestures. A presenter who stays glued to the overhead projector or maintains a white-knuckle grip on the lectern is terrified, and everyone soon knows it. To give the impression of self-confidence, move about the room and use your hands. You may even convince yourself that all is well. Take advantage of your natural gestures, but avoid using one over and over. Some presenters, told that they need to add movement, adopt one gesture—raising an arm, for example—and use it repeatedly. At worst, such programmed gestures send the audience into a hypnotic state; at best, they're distracting. Tailor your gestures to reinforce your point. For instance, by bringing your hands together, you can assure your audience that your proposal "brings it all together." Similarly, you can refer to the ramifications of a problem by tracing ever-widening circles in the air. Because most management presentations involve visual aids, you can add movement by simply pointing out the most important features on the visual. Moving around the room is helpful if it does not deteriorate into the measured pacing of a caged tiger. To guard against moving too much or pacing about, stop each time you make a point. By pausing completely, you emphasize to your listeners the importance of what you are saying.

Control your facial expressions and mannerisms. Although we all know people who say "If you cut off my hands, I wouldn't be able to talk," very few people actually overdo gestures. Facial expressions, on the other hand, are difficult to control and often give an embarrassingly accurate clue as to how you really feel. Beyond checking yourself on videotape, the best way to control facial expressions is to make sure you're comfortable with your material and prepared to respond honestly and openly to any questions. Try to maintain an accessible, open presence. Remember that a smile breaks down barriers. When you smile at someone, he or she generally smiles back. As you talk, show interest in what you're saying. If you're not interested, how can your audience be?

Maintain eye contact. You will lose support faster by staring at your notes, looking only at the visual, or focusing on a spot high on the back wall than by any "mistakes" you may make in the content of your presentation. Similarly, if you direct yourself exclusively to the key decision maker in your audience, he or she will feel more uneasy than flattered, and others in the room will feel unimportant. Unfortunately, some presenters, once they've learned that eye contact can make the difference between persuasion and failure, fix one person after another with a piercing, unwavering gaze until the target looks away in discomfort. Try, at some point in the presentation, to look at each participant with the goal of giving each, in turn, the brief message, "I can see that you grasp what I'm saying." Then, for your own comfort, focus on people who respond with a nod or smile rather than on people who seem bored or hostile.

Establishing Rapport

We've referred a number of times to the need for establishing rapport. There are various ways to do this. For example, people tend to believe those whose background, education, or belief system is similar to their own. Of course, that situation is not likely to occur 100 percent of the time, but you can always find ways to reinforce your common humanity with others. One management presenter we know has an invisible disability (inadequate depth perception) and always tells his audience at the outset that he has been known to trip over the projector cord. Not only does this assertion establish his rapport with anyone in the audience who has ever tripped or been clumsy, but, as he says, it also relieves his anxiety about tripping. If he trips, everyone has a good-natured laugh; if he doesn't, well, he's ahead of the game.

Another way of getting the audience on your side is to use "I," "we," and "you" appropriately. When you're essentially relaying bad news about your department, say "I" and take responsibility for your lack of direction. Don't say "they" and assign blame. (In fact, leave any suggestion of name-calling behind.) If you're presenting the work of a team, share the credit: "we found" or "we suggest." Also, use "we" if you're including the audience in a joint venture such as problem solving or decision making. "You" is ideal for unifying members of the group. When you're saying something that may be obvious to some members of your audience and not to others, you can simply and effectively avoid creating "in" and "out" groups by using the phrase "as you know," and then continuing your statement.

Using Notes Effectively

It's hard to imagine anyone trying to memorize a presentation word for word. Recall takes so much energy that you would have little left for relating to the audience. Worse yet, if you forget a line, you might have to back up all the way to the beginning—every presenter's nightmare. Don't ever consider memorizing. Instead, learn to use notes unobtrusively and effectively.

In a management presentation, using notes is also more effective than reading a script. Although sometimes you may consider reading a speech to an external audience (which we discuss in chapter 9), for an internal presentation, reading is likely to cause the audience to wonder why you didn't simply hand out a report. In addition, you imply that you're insecure about your message. If you know what you're talking about, you should be able to go ahead and say it.

Some people simply must have the full text of the presentation on hand somewhere. It gives them a sense of confidence, even if they never consult it. If you need this "security blanket," keep it out of sight. Too many presenters fiddle with the speech or use it when they gesture. Waving a sheaf of paper at the audience looks more pedagogical than managerial.

If you're forced to substitute for someone at the last moment, read the script, eliminate any purely personal passages, absorb the meaning, and convert it into your own notes. Among other things, this will stop you from repeating the experience of the presenter who, before she realized her mistake, launched energetically into a first-person story about a combat experience as a U.S. Marine.

As mentioned earlier, many management presenters use either their storyboards or their visuals as notes. If your storyboards or visuals are not sufficient to remind you of the details, you can construct notes in several forms. However you do it, they should be easy to use. In terms of content, you should include your opening remarks as well as your ending remarks and any statistical information that is too difficult to remember and will not appear on your visuals. Write down the name of the person who will introduce you and the names of key people in the audience—it's common to block on names when you're under pressure. For long presentations, your notes may go into more detail than is necessary for a short presentation. If you plan to use extensive notes, we suggest you underline key points or create a broad band of color with a highlighting pen that does not obliterate the words beneath. (Remember that these pens work only on typewritten material; handwritten notes in ink will bleed.) In either case, however, never use full sentences because you may lapse into reading them and thus destroy your phrasing.

Two popular notetaking devices are to write simple key words or phrases on index cards or on the frames of your transparencies.

Index cards. Whether you use 3 × 5 or 4 × 6 index cards largely depends on personal preference (and eyesight). A correctly worded note card may look like the one on the next page.

Never walk around holding your index cards. Let them remain on the lectern or the table so that you are free to make assertive gestures without waving your notes around. Furthermore, if they are safely placed, you will not give in to the temptation to hurl them onto the table when you're finished—a most distracting finale.

Transparency frames. If you use overhead transparencies, you can easily jot your notes on the cardboard frames. Generally, the

> To REFOCUS EFFORTS FOR PROFITABLE GROWTH:
>
> - INCREASE VOLUME 15%: UNTAPPED MARKET
>   IN 3 URBAN AREAS
> - CUT COSTS
>   - FIXED: AUTOMATE WAREHOUSE OPERATION
>   - VARIABLE
> - INCREASE PRICE 6%: NOT
>   PRICE-SENSITIVE

transparency carries your major message, especially if it's a text visual, and your notes simply remind you of any further statistical evidence you may want to present. If the main points on the index card exhibited above were used on a transparency, the notes on the border might look like this:

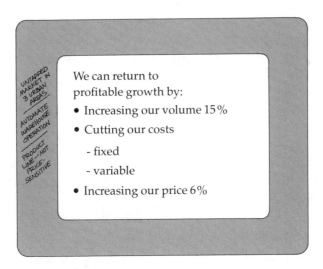

You may want to put sheets of 8½ × 11-inch paper with additional notes between the overheads. The fact that the audience can't see you using such notes makes your delivery smooth and enhances your confidence.

Speaking Clearly

Printed words are separated by spaces. Sentences on the printed page are separated by punctuation marks. Paragraphs are marked by indentations. Since your listeners do not have that kind of visual guidance, they must rely upon you, as the speaker, to enunciate clearly, pause appropriately, provide verbal guideposts (such as "first, second, third"), and offer visual support.

Although rehearsing with a videotape or tape recorder will help you enunciate clearly and without exaggeration, having another person present to react to your rehearsal can help alert you to manners of speech that you may overlook. If you have not had speech training, you may not be aware when you drop endings ("doin'" instead of "doing"); slur words together; fail to pause between words, phrases, and sentences; or pause inappropriately. Be especially careful in pronouncing numbers. Even the most attentive listener can easily mistake "sixteen thousand" for "sixty thousand."

You also help your listeners by varying the rate at which you speak. For complex material, particularly, speak more slowly. If you have studied a foreign language, you know how difficult it is to listen to native speakers conversing at their normal rate (what most non-native listeners want to say is "slow down!"). When you are presenting complex, technical, or unfamiliar (to your audience) material, it is as if you are speaking another language, and most listeners have to shift from "automatic" to "manual" in order to keep up with you. If you persist in moving along at a rapid rate, your audience will tune you out.

You convey confidence when you speak at a moderate volume and pitch. A voice that's too soft is more often the problem than a voice that's too loud (although for some, nervousness leads to higher-than-normal volume). If you are presenting to a large group and using a microphone, ask before you begin whether everyone can hear you or whether your voice is too loud. Vary your pitch as you go along; an even pitch becomes a drone. Lowering your voice is as much an attention-grabber as raising it.

Dealing with Interruptions Gracefully

As you speak, anticipate interruptions by looking for facial cues—better yet, encourage interruption. For example, you might say, "Harold, you look as if you'd like to make a point here . . ." In fact, you may want to let participants know, early in your presentation, that interruptions are welcome. Even if no one offers a comment during the presentation, the idea that it is acceptable establishes a positive, open atmosphere. Permission to interrupt puts the audience at ease and tells your listeners that you have confidence in yourself and your material.

The key to dealing with interruptions is to be brief. Respond to the question and move on. Unnecessary digressions ruin your pace and make it difficult to get the audience back with you. If the question relates to something you intend to discuss later, try to handle it briefly when it comes up and then move on.

Unlike brainstorming sessions, in which it all happens before your eyes, in presentations, you already will have turned up most, if not all, feasible alternatives in the course of your preparatory research. If someone raises an alternative you have rejected, be sure to acknowledge the questioner's intelligence before jumping in to show you have done your homework: "That's a good point. We did look at turnaround times in the Packman Warehouse, however, and found . . ." Never put someone on the spot and never get defensive.

So far, we have talked about normal, comfortable, temporary interruptions. There is another category we might describe as "acts of God." Some are serendipitous—as, for example, when an executive's oration on the folly of deferred maintenance was interrupted by a sudden leak in the conference room. Some are less felicitous—for example, when jackhammers start to rip up asphalt just outside the meeting room window. Don't try to compete with extraneous noise. Move the site of your presentation as gracefully as you can. The delay involved is less costly than fighting what will inevitably be a losing battle.

There are other, equally uncontrollable, interruptions. At least once during your career as a presenter, the ultimate disaster is going to happen. For example, you're halfway through your remarks when a secretary comes into the room and whispers a message to a key person. You are then told you have three minutes to wrap it up before someone must fly to the site of an oil discovery in the North Sea. As long as you've prepared well, you'll be ready. Go to the text visual that sums up your main point and major support points and calmly go over it. Your ability to deal with upsets and surprises of this sort speaks for your managerial skills as well as your skills as a presenter.

Managing the Question-and-Answer Period

Just as you sometimes encourage questions during your presentation, be sure to invite participation when you're finished. Say something simple like, "I'll be glad to answer any questions you have." In some cases, you may want to ask people you know to pose one or two questions just to get the discussion going. Regard this portion of the presentation as a chance to:

- Gather new information
- Stress your main point
- Get commitment to your plan of action

No matter how well you've prepared, someone in the audience may have information you don't have or may contribute something you haven't thought of. Your ultimate goal is to contribute to the success of your organization. Questions, comments, and discussion serve that goal very well. The more people who participate and the more questions they ask, the more effective you're likely to be.

The first step in responding to questions is to listen very carefully. Nod to show that you are paying attention. Don't be surprised if the question has to do with a point you're sure you covered in your presentation. The person may not have understood your comments or may have been distracted at the moment. In addition, you may not have put your point across as clearly as you thought. Remember that the other members of the audience invariably identify with the questioner, not the speaker. To say, "Well, I thought I covered that in my remarks," or to sigh resignedly and roll your eyes, cuts off discussion and damages your credibility with the audience. Some guidelines should help.

Let people finish. The lack of good manners in American society stands out when you compare an interchange among American managers with a similar encounter among people from some other cultures—Asians, for example. Always be polite. Wait until you are sure the person has finished before you answer. If the questioner attempts to dominate with repeated questions, allow him or her to finish a question, respond to it, and then turn to call on someone else. In this situation, some communication consultants recommend looking away from the questioner when you have finished your answer to discourage another question.

Respond to everything, even statements. Many managers feel a need to participate on some level even if they have no question to ask. Their statements do serve a function; in fact, they often register approval of whatever the presenter has said and, as such, are valuable in building consensus for a decision. Merely nodding agreement to such a statement is not enough. Say something like, "Thanks for sharing your point of view with us," or "I agree with you. It's vitally important that we . . ." (which gives you an opportunity to reinforce your main point).

Restate the question. You restate the question not only because others may not have heard it but also to get confirmation from the questioner that you understood it correctly. Because, as with all communications, we process questions in terms of our own expectations, beliefs, and prejudices, it is easy to distort or misinterpret a person's meaning or intent. By restating the question you also give yourself time to think of the appropriate answer. Don't feel rushed. If you pause before you respond, it is a compliment to the questioner, not a sign of indecision. If the question seems loaded—like the stockholder's "Why are the auditors' comments in the annual reports always hedged to the point of meaninglessness?"—restate it in a more neutral form: "The question concerns the specificity of the auditors' notes in the annual report."

Stay on track. Particularly when the question is a long one, it is easy to let boredom, or the fact that the speaker's words have triggered a wholly different thought, distract you. Remember that the question-and-answer period is not a brainstorming session; it is a focused attempt to get agreement and promote action. If the question takes you far afield, answer it, but then bring the discussion back to the subject at hand. For example, you might say "Are there any questions about implementation?" (or an equally specific area germane to your topic).

Admit you don't know the answer. No one expects you to know everything. Frequently, the person who asked the question actually knows the answer and is merely testing to see whether you know it as well. Bluffing in these situations can be immensely harmful. If you don't have the information, say so, and offer to provide the data as soon as possible.

Control the discussion. Unless you're confronting an authoritarian decision maker, don't let any one person dominate the discussion. If someone seems to be asking a series of questions that neither contribute to the discussion nor clarify the topic, pick someone with whom you have rapport and solicit his or her views. Obviously, call only on someone who would welcome the chance to participate. Make sure, too, that everyone has a chance to speak. If another member of the audience interrupts the questioner, intervene. If time is tight, let people know in advance how many questions you can entertain. Then you won't have to antagonize people by cutting them off in the middle of a line of questioning.

Move toward action. The more intense and widespread the discussion after a presentation, the more likely it is that your group will commit itself to a decision. Toward the end of the session, attempt to get closure on the issue by summarizing what you believe to be the group consensus and by tying the consensus to the purpose of your presentation. If you have worked up an implementation schedule that involves members of the audience, this is also the time to get their commitment to it. You can do so simply by asking each person whether he or she has any problems with the assigned task.

Evaluating Your Presentation

When you rehearsed the presentation, you anticipated what could go wrong and sought out your colleagues' advice. After the presentation, you need to evaluate your work. If the experience was unpleasant, you'll probably be tempted to distance yourself and forget it. Although that is a natural reaction, you can learn valuable lessons by carefully reviewing the presentation. If it was videotaped, brace yourself and look at it closely. If not, buttonhole someone who attended and ask very specific questions ("How was it?" leads to unhelpful answers like "terrific"). Use the checklist on page 145 as a guide to what to ask yourself or selected participants.

Naturally, one measure of your effectiveness is reaching the objective you set for your proposal. However, it isn't the only measure or even the most accurate. On the one hand, a previous speaker, circumstance, or event may have "pre-sold" your audience; on the other, your audience may have been so besieged by problems that it would have jumped at any solution. It is equally possible that, despite overwhelming evidence and support for your plan, the key decision maker may choose to follow some flash of insight that has little or nothing to do with your proposal.

Checklist for Evaluating the Presentation

- Did the presentation meet my objective?
- If not, did the discussion lead to a decision close to my fallback position?
- Was I in control of the presentation?
  - —Did I encourage participation?
  - —Did I handle interruptions smoothly and without showing irritation?
  - —Did I answer questions adequately?
  - —Did the audience fidget or seem uncomfortable?
  - —Did I appear to be comfortable throughout? (If not, why not?)

Since the process of gaining acceptance for a major proposal may take months, even years, don't invest too much in the success of one presentation. If you've followed our suggestions so far, you have gotten as far as you can—this time—and you have laid the foundation for continual improvement of your skills.

SUMMARY

Rehearsing increases confidence and improves your delivery:
- Rehearse three times: alone, before a supportive but uninvolved friend, before several co-workers
- Time the presentation and establish a sensible pace

During the presentation:
- Use strong, precise language
- Alleviate nervousness by thinking positively and by establishing rapport with the audience
- Read nonverbal cues in order to
  - —establish the appropriate distance between you and audience
  - —stand and move with confidence
  - —control facial expressions and mannerisms.
- Use notes—on cards, overhead frames, or sheets of paper.
- Be prepared to summarize as necessary
- Respond to questions openly and encourage comments.
- Control the discussion at all times.
- Evaluate each presentation soon after you make it

8

MEETINGS, NEGOTIATIONS, AND INFORMAL CONFERENCES

Many of the techniques for making formal presentations also apply to:
- Participating in meetings
- Negotiating
- Getting action through telephone calls and informal conferences

Participating in Meetings

Many managers hate meetings, often with justification.

"I spend most of my time in meetings; I can't get any work done."

"We listen to the same arguments time after time, and we never make a decision."

"Jim (Jane) blathers on interminably. He (she) doesn't know when to stop."

Meetings, like presentations, are action-oriented. For a meeting to be effective, it must have an objective. By focusing on that objective and using the techniques for developing a logical argument for a specific audience, leaders and participants together move the discussion toward a useful conclusion.

Being the Leader

Chairing a meeting means more than taking the seat at the head of the table. You need to understand your role, assemble a group of people who can take action, make sure that they are properly prepared, keep the discussion focused and moving, and arrange for the implementation of any decisions.

Clarify your expectations. If you're the senior person (the boss chairing the weekly staff meeting, for example), decide and then let people know who will make the final decisions. Although most people these days pay lip service to collegial management styles in which everyone participates in problem solving and decisions are made by consensus, it's unfair to assemble people, suggest that you will accept the decision of the group, and then, if things don't go your way, reserve the decision for yourself. It's far better for everyone to know that the decision is yours than to change the rules in midstream.

Establish the objective. For a meeting to be useful, the discussion must be focused. If you inform the participants in advance about the purpose of the meeting, they can come prepared to contribute. Advance notice does not stifle creativity; instead, it helps get everyone on the same wave length—a necessary step toward using the meeting time to advantage. To state the purpose of the meeting clearly, you need to think about it on two levels. First, in a broad sense, consider where your meeting falls on a continuum between information sharing and decision making—most fall somewhere near the middle. For example, a meeting called to review progress on a project includes sharing information to bring everyone up to date as well as problem solving to deal with both anticipated concerns and anything else that crops up during the discussion. Second, once you know what you want to achieve on a broad scale, decide more specifically what you want to happen as a result of the meeting. The person who calls a meeting, just like a potential presenter, should be able to state the objective clearly in one sentence, as in the following examples:

```
Coordinate division plans for next month's move and
design a contingency.

Decide whether to construct a new plant in South
Carolina.

Review second-quarter sales and make any necessary
changes in third-quarter marketing plan.
```

Each of these statements is specific and complete. In the last example, if the leader had said simply, "Review second-quarter sales," some participants might have assumed that the discussion would focus on adjustments to the third-quarter marketing plan, especially if second-quarter sales had taken a dive, but they would not necessarily have thought about a specific course of action.

Even weekly staff meetings, if they are not to become tedious and unproductive rituals, ought to have objectives. In general, staff meetings should focus on change—that is, on identifying existing problems, anticipating potential problems, or looking for opportunities. Recitals of routine activities, the standard fare of many staff meetings, guarantee boredom and resentment. Regularly scheduled meetings seem to have a life of their own. It's a good practice to think about whether *any* regular meeting is necessary.

Can a meeting have more than one objective? As long as everyone attending has a vested interest in every topic, and as long as you can deal with each topic quickly, meetings with multiple objectives can be successful. (When you circulate your preliminary agenda, doublecheck the level of interest in each topic. If only two people care about an item, delete it from the agenda and have them meet separately.) Keep in mind, however, that problem solving is difficult in a group of more than eight, and no one should be present at a discussion in which he or she has no reason to participate. Furthermore, a person's capacity for unbroken concentration is about 1½ hours. If you know it will take longer than that to reach all your objectives, schedule several short meetings instead of one long one. If the agenda is heavy and people have come from out of town to attend the meeting and can't be re-assembled easily, a meeting may run several hours. In this case schedule a 15-minute break every hour and a half, with refreshments.

Preparing the agenda. The agenda items should relate directly to the meeting's purpose. For example, if the purpose is to "decide whether to recommend adding production capacity in our trimming department," each agenda item should refer to a specific step in the problem-solving process:

```
1.  Establish criteria for decision making
2.  Review five-year production figures
3.  Estimate short- and long-term demand
4.  Review construction cost estimates
5.  Evaluate potential short-term use of excess
    capacity
```

The leader starts the problem-solving process by isolating the pieces of the problem and putting them on the agenda. The agenda items must be so specific that participants can consider the issues in advance and be ready to contribute to the discussion. Notice that in the example above the meeting's purpose calls for a recommendation. Whether you're working alone or as part of a team, to make a recommendation your first order of business is to establish the criteria against which to measure the possible solutions. Therefore, the first item on the agenda is to formulate these criteria.

Selecting the participants. Developing the invitation list for a meeting is an art. On the surface, it is much like drawing up the list of attendees for a presentation: only those people who will participate in making the decision or who have a vested interest in the outcome should attend. But what should you do when you want to invite people whose interest is not great but whose contribution to part of the discussion is valuable? It is insulting to invite someone to provide information and then summarily dismiss him after he has said his piece. If his contribution is worth hearing, he should be invited to stay for the entire discussion. If confidentiality is an issue, schedule another meeting. In a similar vein, if someone with both substantial organizational power and a stake in an issue cancels at the last minute, postpone discussion of that item to another time. More than likely, any decision that's made in that person's absence won't hold and the whole issue will have to be reopened later.

In selecting participants, consider, again, your purpose. The closer your purpose is to the decision-making end of the continuum, the more homogeneous the group should be. No more than two levels in the company's hierarchy should be present if you want the best results. Lots of posturing, but poor problem solving is likely to take place, for instance, in a group that includes the staff, the boss, and the boss's boss. If the meeting is largely designed to share information, the homogeneity of the group is less significant. If the invitation list begins to read like the company's softball league roster, however, go back to the agenda, narrow the objective, and prune some of the topics.

In planning meetings, it is a good idea to keep in mind that most people concentrate best in the morning and like to do their individual thinking early on. Scheduling an important meeting for the middle of the morning breaks into their routine and may spoil their day. The best hour to start an afternoon meeting is about 2:00 P.M. with an ending time of 3:00 or 3:30 P.M. so that participants can go back to the office and handle any pressing matters before they leave for the day. If people are coming from out of town, afternoon meetings or luncheon meetings are preferable to morning meetings to allow for the transportation delays that throw people off schedule.

Determine the order of the agenda. Sometimes the order of agenda items is predetermined by logic; the one mentioned earlier is a good example. If the meeting includes several disparate topics, however, review the public positions of those attending the meeting, or try to divine their preconceived ideas, and deal with less "toxic" agenda items first. If you begin with a subject on which there is general agreement rather than conflict, you are more likely to maintain harmony throughout the meeting.

Decide who should conduct the meeting. If you initiate a meeting, you'll usually also lead it. Sometimes, however, you may choose to delegate the job. If you've called a meeting to consider a problem in which you have a large stake and a strong position, choose a competent person to direct the discussion—one whom other participants view as impartial. At times, a relative outsider may serve as a leader to insure impartiality. For example, someone from the human resources department may lead a meeting in the finance department. Whatever the circumstances, the leader's purpose is to facilitate problem solving or decision making and to keep the discussion on an even keel. He or she is not a participant and should never dominate the meeting. In addition, the leader should understand what contribution each participant can be expected to make and on what issues a consensus must be reached.

Distribute material in advance. The leader should distribute, well in advance of the meeting, a written notice that states the time, the meeting's purpose, the agenda, a list of the participants, and any pertinent written materials (see Exhibit 8.1 for a sample preliminary agenda). The agenda should include a time estimate for each item so that participants can judge the level of detail they're expected to go into. Always include the time the meeting itself will end—people tend to be much more concise when they know the time limits. Some managers like to include on their agenda a synopsis of the decision each item will require. If the group has sufficient trust in the leader, or if the leader has sufficient clout, these directions promote quick closure on each point. Keep in mind, however, that it's rarely possible to achieve enthusiastic, unanimous agreement. As the leader, you must be prepared to accept less than total consensus; that is, you must be satisfied if those present simply agree not to block a decision or if they agree only to try a course of action. Again, if you solicit everyone's point of view but retain the right to make the decision yourself, you must make this clear to the participants; otherwise, they are likely to feel cheated.

Naturally, the leader should give everyone who is expected to make a presentation sufficient lead time to do a credible job of preparing. Less obviously, the leader should alert any participant expected to contribute more than general comments. Failure to let people know that they'll be called on for information in their areas of expertise puts them in an uncomfortable position.

Control the process. Protect the meeting from outside interruptions. Never let people take calls except in cases of dire emergency. Unless you've had problems in the past with how participants related to one another, let people sit wherever they want.

Exhibit 8.1

SAMPLE PRELIMINARY AGENDA

```
                          Preliminary Agenda

Date:      June 17, 1982

Time:      10:00 A.M. to 11:30 A.M.

Location:  Meeting Room B

Objective: Decide whether to recommend additional production capacity
           in trimming department

Attendees: Joe Fischer
           Stan Sussman
           Eric DeRenzie
           Jane Coleman
           Lewis O'Neil
           Betsy Zerlow
```

Agenda Item	Purpose	Allotted Time	Presenter	Material to be read in advance
Establish criteria for making decision	consensus	15 min	--	--
Review 5-year production figures	information	10 min	J.F.	figures
Estimate long- and short-term demands	decision	20 min	J.C.	--
Review cost estimate	information	15 min	S.S.	estimates
Consider potential short-term use of excess capacity	decision	20 min	B.Z.	estimates

Participants usually distribute themselves around the table in a manner that makes them feel relaxed—and their feeling of relaxation usually improves the openness of the discussion. If you do anticipate problems, try to make adjustments so that two people who have strongly opposing views don't sit opposite each other (people are more likely to argue when they can establish good eye contact). One technique is to ask a confederate to station himself opposite one of the antagonists; but this ploy may be excessive except when serious conflict is expected. If the meeting is very formal, it is quite acceptable to provide tent cards that assign seats. If certain participants frequently interrupt with side comments, try to break up the clique by assigning seats or by assigning one of the individuals the task of making a presentation, as long as that presentation makes sense in the context of the meeting. The presenter will be so busy concentrating on his or her presentation that there won't be time for byplay.

As the participants enter the room, try to read any nonverbal cues that give you insight into each person's mood. Although managers pride themselves on their objectivity, they are inevitably influenced by other factors. If you rely on someone who has been a mainstay in the past to carry the discussion when her mind is clearly elsewhere, you may not achieve your goal.

Always start on time. Begin the meeting by restating the purpose (remember, some people may not have read their mail) and guide it to a successful conclusion by insisting on discipline, encouraging participation, summarizing the discussion, and providing transitions between agenda items. During the discussion, don't permit side conversations, in-jokes, innuendos, or anything else that might destroy cohesiveness. To stimulate clearheaded discussion, ask open-ended questions (that is, questions requiring more than a simple yes or no answer). If it would not be threatening to others, you might ask the same question of several participants and point out how their answers compare or contrast. (Of course, you wouldn't actually repeat the question, but rather say, "What would you do in that situation, Charlie?" or words to that effect.) Keep people on track politely but firmly. Should someone begin a major digression, for example, try something like this: "That's an interesting point, but we're getting pretty far afield. Let's get back to the agenda for now and talk about that next week." If discussion of a particular item begins to take much longer than you planned, assign someone to look into it further and report at the next meeting. As we have said, consensus on all items may not always be possible—for instance, if your discussion has turned up information gaps that must be filled or if a conflict is too deep. You should be able to demonstrate consensus on at least some items, however, or participants will leave discouraged. When you reach agreement on an item requiring action, write out what the action is and identify the person responsible (see Exhibit 8.2). At regular intervals

Exhibit 8.2
SAMPLE ASSIGNMENTS SHEET

ASSIGNMENTS

Meeting Objective: DECIDE WHETHER TO RECOMMEND ADDITIONAL PRODUCTION
CAPACITY IN TRIMMING DEPARTMENT

Meeting Date: JUNE 17, 1982

Decision adopted: RECOMMEND ADDITION TO FACILITIES — SIZE TO BE DECIDED.

Action Plans:

Action	Person Responsible	Completion Date
DEVELOP NEW EXHIBITS SHOWING DEMAND BY SECTOR.	J.C.	JUNE 24
PUT TOGETHER TABLE FOR SENIOR MANAGEMENT SHOWING BEST, WORSE, MOST LIKELY CASES	S.S.	JUNE 22

NEXT MEETING SCHEDULED FOR JUNE 25

clarify and summarize to keep participants from ruminating too long on one topic and to help them move on to the next. Properly done, summarizing serves not only as a reminder but also as a way of checking to see that everyone is on the same track. Its function is similar to previewing and reviewing in a presentation.

Always end on time. Don't ever ask the fateful question: Does anyone have anything else to discuss? Someone will, and, chances are, it won't be anything you want to deal with. If you've managed the process appropriately, you'll never have true unfinished business. At the end of the meeting, summarize the discussion, indicate items on which there is agreement, review all the action plans (state the name of the person responsible for implementation and the date by which completion is expected), and thank the participants. After the meeting, you may want to provide additional reinforcement by sending a memo that recalls this information.

To improve your leadership skills, review the meeting in your mind as soon as it ends. Use the following checklist to help you evaluate your performance.

Checklist for Evaluating Yourself as Leader

- Was the agenda appropriate to the purpose?
- Was the meeting timely?
- Was consensus reached on a sufficient number of items?
- Did I prepare participants adequately?
- Was everyone who could provide vital information included?
- Did I encourage participation?
  —Did I cut anyone off too soon?
  —Did I keep people from rambling?
  —Did I call on everyone who wanted to speak?
- Did I let someone else control the meeting? If so, why?

If you lead a group that meets regularly, it is equally important to set aside five or ten minutes at the end of the meeting to discuss how the meeting went. This debriefing lets the group members share their concerns and suggest ways to improve the effectiveness of the process as well as to increase their sense of responsibility.

Being a Participant

A friend of ours has a wonderful poster tacked on her door. It says, "Don't just talk—say something!" It's the best advice we can give to anyone acting as a participant in a meeting. As a participant, your responsibility is to listen actively, to consider new ideas, and, most of all, to make an intelligent and positive contribution.

One way to stay with the topic is to draw on the presentation skills you learned in the earlier chapters. Use an organization tree as a structure for notetaking. If you're lucky, the speaker will open with his or her main point. Write it down and then listen to see how the point is supported. If no main point is apparent, jot down ideas as they're presented and connect them as relationships emerge. This technique forces you to listen critically and to see both the strengths and weaknesses in the argument. A few sessions of listening to illogical or pointless arguments will also teach you to pay attention to your own presentation skills. You'll soon find yourself silently asking "What is my purpose? What is my main point? What is my support?" before you speak.

If you intend to respond with a significant argument rather than a simple comment, quickly sketch a tree to remind yourself of your support points. By getting into the habit of diagramming arguments, you will insure that your contribution to meetings is meaningful. If, for example, your group is reviewing last year's production to estimate expansion needs, and you believe the figures for one item are not representative of production capability because a severe winter and a trucker's strike caused delivery delays, the temptation may be to say: "We shouldn't use these figures. They're not realistic." Far better, however, to stop and ask yourself: "What exactly do I want to accomplish?" and "What do I want these people to do?" Presumably, you want any decision to be based on accurate projections, and you want the participants to accept your view. By knowing what you hope to accomplish, you can avoid fueling a heated personal debate and can concentrate on advancing the discussion.

Once you've decided your remarks will make a contribution, decide how much you absolutely need to say for people to understand your position. In other words, analyze the audience before you make your tree. Then jot down your main point: *We should add 2,000 pieces to the figures.* Your notes might look like this:

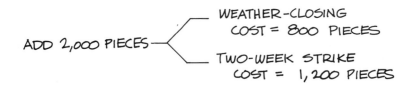

Speak to your main point first. As people begin to think about a rebuttal, they stop listening. Therefore, if you don't make your main point first, they won't hear it. Continue with your support points and then stop. Most of us, once we start talking, rather enjoy the sound of our own voices. Listeners, however, appreciate conciseness. Often, those who say the least at a meeting are listened to most.

Stay until the end. On occasion, agendas are arranged to leave the most controversial items for last on the theory that there will be quicker agreement if only the most interested participants remain. If you find such an item toward the end of the list (and the meeting is running late), try to negotiate a postponement until the next meeting.

During the meeting, concentrate on issues, not on your performance. After the meeting, however, take a few minutes to review the quality of your participation.

Checklist for Evaluating Yourself as Participant

- Did I concentrate on the argument?
- Did I add anything new to the general understanding of the problem or did I "grandstand"?
- Were my contributions stated in positive rather than negative terms?
- Were my remarks complete but concise?

Sometimes the most accurate answers to these questions come from recalling the response you got during the discussion. Too much focus on others' responses, however, can make you overly critical. After all, some personal bias could be motivating another's response. In the long run, you're the best judge of your participation.

Negotiating

So far we've talked about meetings in which, ostensibly, everyone has at least a basic interest in proceeding toward a solution to a problem or in taking advantage of a strategic opportunity. In a negotiation, however, the participants, at least initially, view themselves as adversaries. In other words, they believe the outcome of the discussion will leave one side a winner and one a loser. A great many books talk about winning and losing in negotiations. In almost every case, they advise against openness and trust. Instead, they suggest various methods of making sure you come out the winner.

We suggest that to be successful in a negotiation you apply the problem-solving skills and communication techniques we've been discussing. A positive attitude is the key. Most people are so intimidated by the prospect of confronting a person or a group they believe may be hostile that they lose sight of the fact that these people probably feel the same way about them.

If you find yourself in a situation in which you define the other side as an opponent rather than a colleague (for instance, in a fight over budget allocations), avoid making hard-nosed demands or taking an extreme position. Instead, think in terms of the audience profile and size up the other person's criteria. In fact, a discussion of the criteria is an ideal way to begin a negotiation. Try to settle at the outset how both of you will measure whether a solution is acceptable or not. Often you will find that the other person's criteria are similar to your own or, at least, not in conflict with them. For example, in negotiating budget allocations, one person may want his or her allocation for production to be commensurate with that in other firms and, to that end, cite an average figure of $2.6 million. You, on the other hand, may want to allocate $750,000 to research and development to keep that division in the forefront, but you are willing to give a little in other areas. These criteria may not be in conflict, but you'll never know until you get them out in the open. Furthermore, the very act of getting agreement on criteria may help set a conciliatory tone when you negotiate more substantive points.

Once you've determined the other side's criteria, talk about your options. Never back anyone into a corner by insisting that he or she take a position for or against an issue. Instead, try to spell out as many options as you can, being sure to include some that meet your opponent's important criteria.

Consider how you would negotiate a raise with your boss. If you flatly demand a 15 percent raise without any attempt at discussion, she is far more likely to say no than if you open the discussion by trying to get agreement on at least some of the criteria. Then you have a basis for establishing the general principle that you deserve additional compensation. Once you are in agreement, you can discuss what form it should take: a raise, a bonus, or some other option. Remember, people are more interested in meeting their own criteria than in meeting yours.

In essence, then, a sensible negotiator, while recognizing the potential for conflict, relies on an audience profile and problem-solving techniques to reach agreement. At the same time, he or she tries to focus on the participants' common ground rather than their disagreements. In summary, keep these points in mind as you negotiate:

- Consider what the others want
- Discuss both sets of criteria—yours and theirs
- Consider all the options
- Don't force anyone to take a stand
- Be prepared with a fallback position

Getting Action through Informal Conferences

Telephone calls and short conferences that take place either in the hall or in someone's office are by far the most common form of management communication. Individuals differ in the way they choose to communicate—some people are more effective in person than they are on the phone, whereas others view the telephone as an extension of their right arm. Too often, though, people make the mistake of launching into a discussion or reaching for the phone without thinking through what they want to accomplish. "Thinking on your feet" is a skill everyone admires, but wise managers try to avoid relying on it.

The strategy for both unplanned meetings and phone calls is similar to that for more formal presentations. Start with some preliminary questions such as those in the checklist below.

Checklist for an Informal Conference

- What do I want to accomplish?
- Am I talking with the person who can make that happen?
- Is a phone call or face-to-face conversation best?
- What does the person know about the situation?
- What preconceived ideas might he or she have?
- Do I need any data before I go into this discussion?

Once you've decided it's appropriate to go ahead with the conversation, organize your ideas, just as you would for any presentation. Consider this transcript of a phone call between Joe Seymor, the comptroller for the Midwest division of a manufacturing company, and Jane Thomas, the head of corporate planning. After some initial pleasantries, Joe began:

> Listen, you know we've been having this problem in District five. Well, I was talking to Brette the other day—you know her—she's the one who started in corporate personnel and now does something in human resources for the eastern division. She said she knows some consultants who have a lot of experience with that sort of problem. She thought I should call them. Before I do that, though, I want to check with you.
> [Silence, while Jane wonders: What is "this" problem? Why do I care who Brette is? Who does he mean by "some" consultants? What is he checking with me about? WHAT DOES HE WANT FROM ME?]

Joe committed two major errors: he left out important information, and he told Jane a good deal she didn't need to know. This vagueness and lack of preparation, although common in telephone calls, is nonproductive. Had Joe organized his thoughts and asked himself before he made the call, "What do I want Jane to do?" and "What is my objective?" this call would have proceeded quite differently. Joe's objective would have been to request approval to hire a writing consultant for the senior staff in District five. His notes would have looked like this:

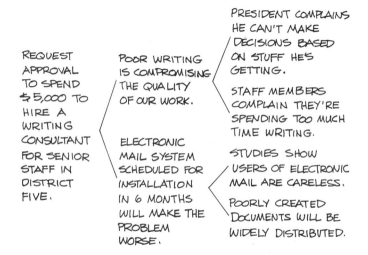

REQUEST APPROVAL TO SPEND $5,000 TO HIRE A WRITING CONSULTANT FOR SENIOR STAFF IN DISTRICT FIVE.

POOR WRITING IS COMPROMISING THE QUALITY OF OUR WORK.

ELECTRONIC MAIL SYSTEM SCHEDULED FOR INSTALLATION IN 6 MONTHS WILL MAKE THE PROBLEM WORSE.

PRESIDENT COMPLAINS HE CAN'T MAKE DECISIONS BASED ON STUFF HE'S GETTING.

STAFF MEMBERS COMPLAIN THEY'RE SPENDING TOO MUCH TIME WRITING.

STUDIES SHOW USERS OF ELECTRONIC MAIL ARE CARELESS.

POORLY CREATED DOCUMENTS WILL BE WIDELY DISTRIBUTED.

Making notes before picking up the phone is absolutely necessary, particularly in the game of telephone tag, in which you and your target keep missing each other's calls. Then, when the person finally reaches you, you most likely have your mind on something else. If enough time has passed, you even may have forgotten why you called. Worse, you may not remember who the person is. An abbreviated tree, on a scrap of paper taped to the phone, will help you enormously. Should you need or want a record of the discussion, you can add to your notes during the return conversation.

Face-to-face conversations often go the same way as unplanned phone conversations—filled with vague references, lacking a proper beginning to orient the listener, and rambling on without clearly disclosing the purpose of the conversation. When you corner a person without warning, it is especially important that you follow the rules for a good beginning and a well-organized argument. Your listener has no idea what to expect and no time to reconstruct past events. If you are buttonholing a person who works in another department and doesn't know you well, the best way to start is by introducing yourself and mentioning your title or function.

Obviously, you would not approach an informal face-to-face conversation with notes in hand. At the same time, it is unwise to have an important conversation if you haven't planned it. But if caught off guard and you can't play for time, keep these guidelines in mind:

- Limit the discussion to those topics that will help you reach your objective.
- In choosing what to say and the order in which to say it, remember the listener's preconceived ideas and knowledge of the subject.
- Be concise.
- Ask questions if you don't understand.

When you get in the habit of following these guidelines, your conversations, both in person and on the phone, should be more fruitful and more efficient.

SUMMARY

To present your views effectively:
- In meetings
  —polish your leadership skills
      establish an objective
      prepare a concise agenda
      select participants carefully
      control the meeting effectively
      distribute advance material
      start and end on time
      summarize and debrief the participants
  —be an active participant
      follow the discussion attentively
      concentrate on issues
      be open to new ideas
      consider your responses before speaking
      make constructive contributions
- In negotiations
  —begin with the criteria
  —consider all the options
  —leave yourself a fallback position
- In telephone calls and face-to-face conferences
  —plan ahead
  —clarify your purpose
  —focus on your objective
  —consider your listener's preconceived ideas and knowledge
  —be concise

SPEAKING OUTSIDE
THE ORGANIZATION

As you rise in the organization you'll have more and more opportunities to address outside groups. To do this effectively you should know how to:

- Adapt your presentation techniques
- Write and read a speech
- Serve on a panel
  —as moderator
  —as panelist

Most presenters find speaking to strangers (that is, anyone outside the organization) much more difficult than speaking to co-workers or other "insiders." In part, this anxiety results from a fear of being misrepresented. We all know people who have been hurt professionally because they were misquoted or their remarks were taken out of context. In large part, though, the uneasiness has a legitimate basis. An organization's culture is sufficiently unique that a great deal of translation and explanation may be required for people not intimately familiar with the organization to understand its actions. No one likes to be evaluated from an uninformed or biased perspective. No wonder, then, that apprehension increases in direct proportion to the amount of hostility a manager expects or the degree of controversy that surrounds a topic.

Except in unusual circumstances, however, making presentations to outside groups should be a satisfying experience. At any rate, it's a skill that all managers have to develop, especially if they hope to attain executive status. CEOs, for example, spend much of their time communicating with people outside the organization. Much of their effort involves dealing with peers in other organizations or negotiating with people in government for example, and they often address large groups at stockholders' meetings, press associations, or trade conventions. Indeed, you undoubtedly will have to confront some external audiences long before you reach the ranks of top management.

Giving an External Presentation

Although most management presentations involve no more than eight to ten people, when you speak to outside audiences you will be addressing larger groups. For the most part, preparation, organization, and rehearsals for these occasions require techniques similar to those we've discussed in earlier chapters. You'll still have to focus on one main point and support it with logical arguments, and you'll still use an open, objective businesslike tone. The greatest adjustment you'll have to make will not be in content or approach, but in your delivery style. Although you should be yourself, you'll have to project your personality with a bit more theatricality and energy when you speak to a large group in an echoing auditorium than when you talk to a small group in a conference room. The following guidelines will help you make a successful external presentation.

"Warm up" the audience. When you make an internal presentation to people you know well, you don't have to spend time "warming up" the group. In an external presentation you'll have to take time for the preliminaries. Starting with an anecdote or a story provides a good introduction. If you have a regional accent that is markedly different from most of the people in the audience, or if English is your second language, make sure you give the audience time to become familiar with your speech patterns before you launch into your main point.

Assert your authority. When you speak before an audience, people expect you to exercise the authority that comes with the role of "expert." Apologies, slumping shoulders, and poor posture all signal a lack of confidence. And, when a speaker appears ill at ease, most listeners let their minds drift rather than vicariously experience the speaker's discomfort. Others may take signs of nervousness as an opportunity to attack. Either way you lose. The opposite problem, pomposity, assuming that your high position in some organization entitles you to a hearing, is equally dangerous. Your success in speaking to outside groups must stem from your personal qualities and expertise more than from your role. No audience will accept what you say if you don't inspire respect and trust. In an external situation, stimulating these feelings in the audience is as important as what you say.

Don't depend on visual aids. Unless you are making a professionally orchestrated performance, such as an address to a stockholders' meeting, using visuals has serious drawbacks in external settings. First of all, any mistakes you make in manipulating the visuals will seem more important than in an internal presentation. Second, the professional standards for visual aids in a public presentation are much higher than in an internal situation. They signal how much both you and your organization care about the impression you're creating. If you don't have a corporate art department, don't even consider visuals. Third, only slides are appropriate for large groups—and that's a drawback because no one can see you in the dark and you won't be able to command much attention. A lighted lectern does not really solve the problem because the general effect is that of a child holding a flashlight under his chin at Halloween.

Use gestures. When you can't move about freely (in many formal situations, you will find the microphone permanently attached to the lectern), gestures are the only way to hold the audience's interest and relieve your own physical tension. Used well, they intensify the meaning of whatever you say. Paradoxically, people who find gestures easy to use in small groups often freeze in front of a large audience. They feel "everyone is looking at me" rather than "everyone is listening to me." As we have recommended previously, any time you find your energy invested more in nervousness than in the content of your talk or your audience, try to find a way to make your anxiety work for you. In this case, you can discharge some of your tension through gestures.

Most new presenters are aware that their usual gestures are too small in scale for a large auditorium or banquet room, but they do not know how to scale them upward. Here are some simple do's and don'ts:

Do . . .
- Gesture with your whole arm rather than your hand and wrist. By using the whole arm, you'll make your gestures more forceful and they'll be more visible from the back of the hall.
- Gesture with both hands. When you use both hands, you appear more confident (because you seem more in control of your body) and more expansive. To improve your use of gestures, notice how professional presenters handle themselves when they address a large group. Then evaluate yourself on videotape.

Don't . . .
- Assume a relaxed, hands-in-the-pockets pose. It's too easy to play with keys or loose change (besides, you'll look like a kangaroo).
- Park your hands on your hips (you'll remind people of their sixth-grade teacher).
- Clasp your hands behind your back (you'll look like a deacon).

Make yourself heard. When you're not accustomed to addressing large audiences, the tendency is to start off too softly, inviting petulant cries of "louder" or "we can't hear you" from the back of the room. These kinds of interruptions diminish your authority in the eyes of the audience. The secret is to test the strength of your speaking voice before the event begins, preferably with a colleague and in the room in which you will speak. After a few trial runs, you'll become comfortable with a tone and pitch that, at first, may have felt unnatural. Practice will also give you an opportunity to work on projecting your voice. If you have any doubt about whether people can hear you, ask the audience if your voice is reaching the back of the room. If you're using a microphone, before the audience arrives, test how far you can move away from it and still be within range. It may be farther than you think. Although inexpensive microphones can't pick up a voice more than eight inches away, professional equipment has a greater range. If you are going to use a lavalier, practice with it ahead of time.

Use eye contact effectively. In large groups, obviously, you cannot look at everyone. But you can look at a group of individuals in each section of the room to assure everyone that you are aware of their presence. It's not an acceptable compromise to look over everyone's head and gaze at some spot halfway up the back wall. Some presenters think this makes the entire audience feel included, but, more likely, it gives people the impression that something in the rear of the room is more important than they are. A perfunctory effort at eye contact is not sufficient. You cannot cast sidelong glances at individuals or make a series of darting eye movements without unsettling the audience. The only kind of eye contact that successfully establishes the feeling of connection with members of the audience is a reasonably long, in-focus look at specific individuals. It may be difficult, at first, to deal with a sea of faces. (Some people actually feel lightheaded the first time they speak in a crowded auditorium.) Eye contact can help to ground you and to eliminate the fantasy of a hostile, threatening mob. You'll find it immensely helpful to look for someone in the crowd you know. If you can't station a supportive friend in one of the first few rows, look at the person who introduced you as you thank him or her, and then turn your attention to finding someone responsive out in the room.

Use notes. Even though the solemnity of the occasion may seem to justify it, we recommend that you do not read a prepared speech unless you are dealing with a highly controversial issue and your remarks may be reported in the press. When you use notes, you indicate that you are in control of the material and have no need to be overly careful about what you say.

Don't use alcohol or relaxants. Although alcohol provides an initial "high," it may make you feel unpleasantly out of control and anxious, encouraging you to be flip and inducing you to make inappropriate remarks. If you drink far enough in advance of the presentation, the ultimate depressant effect will damage your ability to speak forcefully and can play havoc with your timing. In any case, the self you feel internally will be at odds with the one you are projecting to your audience—a dangerous state. Relaxants slow you down and make it difficult to speak resolutely or respond to questions with wit and intelligence, skills very important in external presentations. If dinner is served just before the presentation, avoid eating heavily (perhaps not too difficult, given the quality of most catered meals). Too much food will make you sleepy.

Level with your audience. In external presentations, there may be occasions when hedging is legitimate (if the questioner is overtly hostile, for example, or the facts as currently known suggest one conclusion, but you know that additional information, which is not public, points to another). Sometimes, stung by loaded questions and lulled by the certainty that no one could possibly check it out, presenters are tempted to falsify the facts. Don't succumb to this temptation. Once you are caught distorting the truth, everything you say will be open to question. In short, you'll lose all credibility with this audience, and with future audiences, especially if the press is around to record your misstep. Even if you're not "found out," it isn't worth the anxiety of thinking you might be.

Be open in answering questions. The best way to avoid blurting out something when you're on the defensive is to train yourself to pause before you answer any question. It's perfectly acceptable to say you don't know (if you don't). It's also acceptable to say, "I don't have those figures with me." If it's important enough, you might offer to find the answer or have someone on your staff find it. The person asking the question then has a channel for getting the information later.

If you can't avoid an answer, and the answer may seem damaging, always put the response in context. For example, one speaker pointed out before she responded to a question, "There's a tendency for people to believe there's a solution for every problem. If we could just sit down together, they say, we could work it out. I'm here to tell you, though, that most problems can't be solved—the best we can do is try to make the consequences of the problem less negative." Don't be trapped into answering a request for "a simple yes or no answer"—almost nothing is that simple. By taking something to its logical limits, you can show the absurdity of either/or thinking.

Look for logical flaws, not to embarrass the questioner but to deflect the question. For example, we heard one speaker respond to a loaded question by saying, "I can't agree with you because I don't agree with your major premise, which is that all oil companies are dishonest in reporting their profits."

If you're truly concerned that your audience will be unfriendly, get a friend to role play the question-and-answer period with you. If you've heard a question before, you'll be much calmer when you respond.

Finally, don't get angry and don't lose your sense of humor. One speaker, after a barrage of leading and hostile questions, finally paused, looked at the last person to offer a question, and said, "Could you rephrase that? I haven't got it in a form I want to answer yet."

Writing a Speech

If you must read a speech, take special care to write it or have it written to be spoken, and then prepare to read it carefully.

Use short sentences (no more than two lines) and don't load your prose with convoluted phrases or passive constructions. One new CEO, whose command of the English language had been honed by years of academic training, was in the midst of reading a lengthy sentence in his text when he suddenly stopped and said: "I don't know how I got into this thought, but I sure as hell am willing to admit that I don't know how to get out of it." It was amusing, but the situation was entirely avoidable had he written the words to be spoken, not read. The following guidelines will help you write a readable speech.

Choose simple sentences. Impromptu speakers don't usually load up their sentences with a great many dependent clauses. It's hard to visualize a manager running into an office shouting, "The Thomas computer file, on which I was working 30 minutes ago, has been erased!" More likely you would hear something like "I was working on the Thomas file just thirty minutes ago, and now it's been erased." You may also freely eliminate "that" in sentences like: "It's conceivable that we'll be in the black by 1984." Better yet, just write "I predict we'll be in the black by 1984."

Use verbs rather than nouns. Rather than "there's a belief among managers that," it is more effective and less wordy to say "managers believe that."

Eliminate long connecting words. Most people never use words like "nevertheless," "furthermore," "additionally," and "therefore" when they speak. Including them in a speech meant to be read will distance you from your audience. Substitute "that's why" or "so" for "therefore" or "thus"; "but" or "all the same" for "however" or "nevertheless"; "then" or "and" for words like "furthermore."

Emphasize your ideas with repetition. Consider the strength of this phrasing: "Why should we adopt this budget? Because it's fair. Because it's feasible. And because it's going to guarantee us a competitive edge for the next four years." Repetition of the structure allows the speaker to build the case. Parallel structure, common in written reports, is even more powerful when the words are spoken.

Duplicate the wording of spoken speech. Use short, simple words. Use contractions. Use "I" when appropriate and "you" whenever you can. Leave prepositions and clauses at the ends of sentences. Use everyday words.

Don't be afraid to suggest you're in command. Most people eliminate the appearance of giving orders from their writing. As a speaker, however, you're in charge, and you'll need to maintain that role by providing the audience with guidance. Give your ideas maximum impact by saying, "Think about that for a minute" or "Remember, we've been working on this idea for two years" or "Your support is vital to the success of this plan."

Ghostwriting a Speech

If you're the ghostwriter, make sure you talk frequently and pointedly with the person who will give the speech, and then follow all the rules for good speechwriting. Writing for someone else requires talking with that person long enough to get a sense of his or her speech patterns and vocabulary so the final product will sound like that person, not like you. Even if someone else has given you the assignment, consult with the ultimate consumer. You are inviting disaster if you operate with third-hand information.

From the beginning, make sure that you and the speaker both agree on the main point of the speech. Make a diagram of the argument and get preliminary agreement on it. That way, you can keep a coherent focus even when the person giving the speech tries to throw in irrelevant ideas. Most people are insecure about having someone else write for them—not only is there a great deal of anxiety involved in giving a speech, but also people have an intense ego involvement with the content of the speech itself. If the speech is important enough, the person giving it certainly will talk to many other people to confirm that he or she is on the right track. Each of those people will have suggestions (almost no one who's asked for advice refuses to give it, even if he or she has nothing original to say). Your task is to make sure that, at least while you're still responsible for the product, nothing extraneous is included merely because it "sounds like a good idea." You need not be stubborn or insist on your own ideas over those of the person giving the speech; rather, you need to work with the person either to find a logical way to include the idea or to persuade him or her to hold the idea for another occasion.

Finally, find out who is making the arrangements for the speech itself and, when you deliver the final version of the speech, include a summary of those arrangements as well as the name of the person responsible. If you're the only person with whom the speaker has talked, he or she may incorrectly assume you're in charge of the whole effort. It's far better to dispel this illusion in the beginning than to explain later that you weren't responsible for some misadventure.

Guidelines for Ghostwriting

- Follow the rules for writing a speech.
- Consult frequently with the person giving the speech about
  —audience analysis
  —the main point
  —the organization
  —the tone
- Hold to the line of argument if irrelevant ideas are introduced.
- Don't substitute your ideas for those of the speechmaker.
- Make sure the person giving the speech knows who's responsible for arrangements.

Reading a Written Speech

Review every written speech by reading it aloud and taping it. If you stumble over certain passages, stop. Then put what you're trying to say into simple phrases.

Once the speech is typed (either double or triple space), underline or highlight to indicate stress or emphasis points and to mark pauses. Even if you wrote it yourself, rehearse by reading the speech several times. If someone else wrote it for you, this step is especially important. Nothing is more damaging than reading a speech in such a stilted way that the audience thinks you're seeing it for the first time.

If you work with a speechwriter, make sure you talk to the person several times first. You want to convey not only some sense of your position on the subject but also a sense of your vocabulary and the cadence of your speech. If the speech doesn't sound like you, you won't be able to read it with grace, no matter how much you rehearse. You can save yourself time by talking with the speechwriter at length—before he or she outlines the speech, after you've read the outline, and after you've read the first draft.

In the last analysis, quality control is your responsibility, even if someone else wrote the speech. We were once told a marvelous (if apocryphal) story about President Lyndon Johnson, who decided that he no longer needed his "Rose Garden" speechwriter—the person who wrote routine speeches welcoming groups like Scouts or Texas constituents at informal gatherings in the White House Rose Garden. He gave the speechwriter his pink slip along with a final assignment. On his last day, the speechwriter delivered note-cards for the speech to President Johnson, who strode out to the Rose Garden, welcomed the assembled delegation, and started to read:

```
My fellow Americans:

Some say we cannot have full employment and a low
rate of inflation.

I believe we can and I will tell you how . . .
```

Some say we cannot have true equality of treatment
and a society that rewards merit.

I believe we can and I will tell you how . . .

Some say we cannot protect our national security
and open the door to negotiations with the Soviet
Union.

I believe we can and I will tell you how . . .

LBJ then flipped to the fourth card, which read:

```
Okay, Lyndon, you're on your own.
```

The rest of the cards in the pack were blank.

Serving on a Panel

Executives are often called upon to moderate or participate in panel discussions. Some of the techniques you use in these situations differ from the usual presentation techniques.

Moderating a Panel

As a moderator, you are the leader of the group and, even though you are required to remain in the background far more than when delivering a presentation, you are responsible for attending to a number of seemingly minor but crucial details.

Pay attention to people's names. Although most people, to be polite, laugh off mispronunciations of their names, they often hide their true feelings of offense. This basic reminder may seem simplistic, but even professionals seem to need it. Fred Friendly, moderating a four-member panel on William F. Buckley's television program, "Firing Line," once managed to murder the names of every panelist except Buckley. Once you've got the names right, memorize them. It's good insurance to also have all the names written down somewhere. However, don't read off cards. Doing so signals the audience that the panelists are not particularly important to you—and therefore needn't be to them.

Introduce yourself and the panel members. In your concern for others, it's easy to forget yourself. A simple, "Good afternoon, I'm Harry Newsom, the moderator of our panel on changes in corporate planning policies" is usually enough. In introducing other members of the panel, use the same guidelines we established in Chapter 6. Don't get carried away describing a person's credentials. Confine your remarks to the panelist's expertise on the subject of the discussion.

Set the stage. A good moderator, like a good presenter, creates an appropriate environment for the panel discussion at the outset. Tell the audience what the panel is about, why it is important, and what the format will be. Your tone, your manner, and your professionalism set standards for the panelists and establish rapport with the audience.

Set time limits. It is good practice to note in the beginning the importance of adhering to a schedule. (One moderator complimented each panelist when he or she finished on time.) The wise moderator will set up, in advance, some system for cuing the participants that their time is up and will make sure that everyone understands the ground rules. If a panelist does start to run over, you will need to intervene with some comment like, "We appreciate your detailed discussion, but we need to move on to Mr. Thomas." If you don't control garrulous panelists, tension will start to build in the audience, among the panel members, and particularly in the person who will speak next.

In most cases, it works best to take questions after each panelist has completed his or her remarks. If you ask the audience to hold questions until the end, you run the risk of people forgetting what they want to ask or, worse yet, of people spending the entire presentation "stuck" on their questions. Your job as a moderator also includes limiting the time spent on questions and answers. The early and final remarks tend to get the majority of questions so your greatest problem will be to elicit remarks during the middle.

Maintain a sense of dignity. Even if you know all the members of the panel on intimate terms, the audience does not. "Chatting them up," as one British manager describes it, can devalue the whole enterprise. One moderator, for example, obviously revved up by a particularly intense discussion, signaled the next panelist by saying, "Well, Mike, are you ready to whip it on us?" To some, the phrase sounded quaintly informal, but to many it was offensive. It's far better to be straightforward in your transitions from one speaker to the next and to save informal remarks and in-jokes for another situation.

Provide transitions. A typical transition statement links the speakers together. For example, "Thank you, Ray. Mike Stern will now tell us how the internal auditing system Ray described compares with similar systems in the Midwestern region." Be specific. Rather than say, "Mr. Anthony will now talk about the financial implications," say, "Mr. Anthony will now explain how this proposal will affect the standard of living of most Americans."

Know how to close. If a controversy is raging at the end of a discussion, try to start "decompressing" the participants about five minutes before the time is up. You can do this either by switching to a less controversial topic or by starting to summarize each person's point of view on the issue. At the very end, allow yourself time to make a general summary and a concluding statement. Then thank the panelists for their participation.

Participating in a Panel Discussion

As a participant, you have a responsibility to yourself, to the panel, and to your organization. Although you are only one member on a panel, you still make a presentation whenever you make a statement. Therefore, all the presentation rules apply. Follow these guidelines as well to help you participate with quality.

Remember that you are on stage at all times. The behavior of the panelists, even those who are not speaking, sets the standard for the audience's behavior. Members of the panel often tire of looking at the speaker, and their gaze wanders or they stare into space. That is disconcerting to the audience and to the speaker. Attentive observers in the audience check the panelists' gestures, facial expressions, and posture. They deliberately look for unspoken disagreements or conflicts. You can assist the speaker by being an active listener. Look at the person speaking, nod or smile at the appropriate points, keep an open, easy expression, and take occasional notes to show your attentiveness.

Avoid sending negative messages. First of all, don't show boredom by examining your nails, tugging on your hair or earrings, closing your eyes, sighing heavily, or yawning. (It's rare to see a panelist actually fall asleep, but it has happened.) Also, don't show your hostility with flashing eyes, rigid posture, or a glare at the speaker. The lack of control reflects on you.

Create your own transitions. Sometimes the moderator doesn't provide a transition. In this case, create your own transition. Generally, it's easier to build on whatever the preceding speaker said than to try to provide a transition to the person who follows you. You can usually draw upon some thread in the previous speaker's remarks and show how it relates to what you're going to say.

Be neat. Decline coffee, especially if offered in foam or paper cups. It's far too easy to tip one of these over, and the embarrassment isn't worth it. Water is relatively safe. An audience interprets smoking as a sign of nervousness or mental fatigue and many people resent the haze and odor.

In general, serving on a panel, like delivering any other external presentation, presents you with an opportunity to sell both yourself and your organization. It's something you can (and should) learn to do with style and grace if you're going to advance in the organization.

SUMMARY

Delivery of a presentation to an external audience—stockholders, customers, community groups, the press—though unnerving for the first few times, eventually becomes exhilarating. To be successful, you'll want to

- Adjust your delivery style and, specifically:
  —warm up your audience
  —assert your authority
  —use gestures
  —make yourself heard
  —use eye contact effectively
  —avoid using alcohol or relaxants
  —level with the audience
- Write a speech to be spoken, and read it naturally
  —use verbs instead of nouns

—use everyday spoken language
—emphasize ideas with repetition
- Serve on a panel effectively
  —as a moderator
    set the tone
    provide transitions
    summarize
  —as a participant
    avoid sending negative messages
    create transitions

10

VIDEOCONFERENCES

Videoconferences are already replacing some face-to-face meetings, and, as a manager, you can expect someday to both orchestrate and participate in them. To take full advantage of the opportunities offered by this medium, you'll first need to know how it works, and then how to:

- Decide when a videoconference is appropriate
- Prepare for a videoconference
- Manage the technology and the people as conference leader
- Make an effective contribution as a participant

Numerous corporations have already made a substantial financial commitment to videoconference facilities, and many of them have ambitious plans to expand in the future. Even those not yet willing to create their own studios are renting commercial studios to see what the videoconference has to offer.

The Technology

Because of the wide variety of videoconference forms, recent publicity in the business press has not yet dispelled the confusion videoconference terminology creates among nontechnical managers. "Teleconferencing," the term picked up and popularized by the press, encompasses any form of electronically assisted communication, including electronic mail systems (EMS) and audioconferences, which are simply new, dignified versions of conference calls. "Videoconference," in the sense we're using the word here, can include anything from an audioconference supplemented by slow-speed facsimile transmission, through freeze-frame or slow-scan black-and-white or color video (in which a television picture of either the whole room or only the person speaking is transmitted at a speed ranging from every 20 seconds to every 2 minutes), to full-motion black-and-white or color video with any number of accompanying aids, such as electronic blackboards or computer interfaces. (When someone writes on an electronic blackboard, the writing appears at the other location simultaneously. Conventional "whiteboards" are also used—a presenter simply writes on the board with a magic marker, while a camera zooms in on the characters.) For any conference, several locations may have identical equipment or one may be able to transmit more information than another, as in a one-way video, two-way audio set-up.

In-house or Outside Facilities?

Any corporate management wanting to experiment with videoconferences has at least three choices—constructing in-house facilities, renting equipment to use on the premises, or contracting to use outside facilities. In-house facilities are expensive to construct and maintain. So far, it's impossible to come up with an "average" price because individual requirements for rooms and equipment vary so widely and because the technology is changing so rapidly. Today a freeze-frame conference facility may cost $100,000 whereas a studio capable of producing a full-motion color videoconference can cost in the neighborhood of $1 million (which covers only capital costs for the necessary two or three cameras, video monitor, video recorder, facsimile transmission machines, and satellite earth station). The substantial transmission costs involved in holding full-motion videoconferences depend on the distance between locations and the duration of the meeting.

Executives responsible for in-house videoconference facilities believe that managers are more likely to use this medium when the facility is on site than when they must arrange for outside services. In addition, they believe that having in-house equipment, because it allows participants to rehearse presentations beforehand, improves the quality of a videoconference. Security is also of less concern when videoconference facilities are in-house. Although "scramblers" may be employed to encode and then decode messages, using outside facilities inevitably involves dealing with nonaffiliated technicians and camerapersons, and their presence increases participants' concern about information leaks.

Some companies have chosen to rent videoconference equipment, installing it in-house on a semipermanent basis. Leased equipment is believed to be less reliable, however, than permanently sited equipment. On the other hand, with leased equipment, if the state of the art changes drastically, the equipment contract can be cancelled; money invested in a permanent facility is a sunk cost.

As an alternative to owning or renting equipment for in-house use, an organization can rent videoconference facilities off premises. (Several major hotel chains provide facilities for one-way video, two-way audio meetings.) The corporation or organization seeking to hold the videoconference can then have one of its own people make the technical arrangements or call one of several companies in the business of setting up audio or videoconferences. These companies arrange for satellite time, and will usually also perform some standard housekeeping functions, such as checking visuals to see that they are in order.

Another possibility is using facilities that are permanently staffed and maintained by a group like AT&T's Picturephone™ Meeting Service. AT&T currently has 11 such videoconference rooms in major cities and an ambitious schedule for opening new facilities every year. The cost of renting this set-up is fairly low.

Studio Design

Although present equipment is complex and room arrangements have not been standardized, people with experience in television

and concern for human factors are beginning to design videoconference studios that will assure maximum efficiency and comfort
for participants. For example, it appears that most people respond
better to color television monitors than to black-and-white sets,
presumably because color television is the norm today. In addition,
participants feel more relaxed when they see the entire room at the
other location than when they see only a close-up shot of the person talking, as is the case in a freeze-frame videoconference. It is
even better when the two rooms are similar enough to look like
extensions of each other. Because people tend to "freeze" when
they see a camera or a microphone, it's desirable to hide both these
items.

Exhibit 10.1 shows the room layout used for all Aetna Life &
Casualty Insurance Company videoconferences. This arrangement
is close to ideal—participants at each location are seated; the rooms
are mirror images of each other; the cameras are hidden; and the
console that controls the electronics is easy for the leader to use.
Although they do not guarantee success, such accessible and well
designed facilities help to make a videoconference work well.

Deciding When a Videoconference Is Appropriate

No one holds a videoconference on the spur of the moment,
even if the equipment is available. Any electronic meeting must be
carefully planned. For a videoconference in particular,

- The purpose must be suited to the available technology
- The costs—in time, money, and human energy—must be
  justifiable
- The key people must be willing and able to participate

Is the Purpose Suitable?

Many videoconference veterans are convinced that people reach
better decisions more quickly during a videoconference than when
they are in a conventional meeting. Just as many feel people do *not*
participate because they don't want to prolong the agony. But not
even the most ardent advocates of the office of the future claim
that electronic meetings will replace face-to-face meetings for *all*
purposes.

Problem-solving meetings. Since problem solving is a major
component of most business meetings, the usefulness of video-

Exhibit 10.1
TELECONFERENCE STUDIO — AETNA LIFE & CASUALTY COMPANY

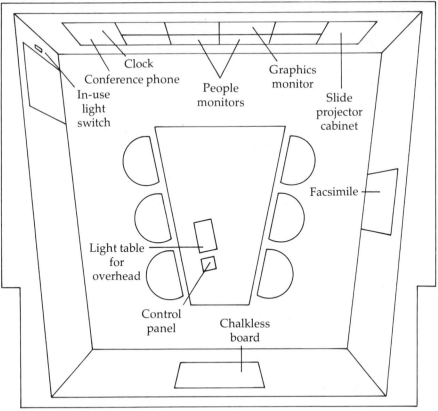

Photograph and schematic drawing used with the permission of AETNA
Life & Casualty Company.

conferences for this purpose is a major concern. Participants accustomed to conferences using full-motion two-way video report that once they adjust to the limitations imposed by electronic conversation, both problem solving and decision making are quite possible in a videoconference setting. Some even believe that the constraints of the medium—rigid time limits imposed by demand for the facilities or the high costs of running overtime—create a healthy discipline that could improve conventional face-to-face meetings.

Some managers argue that videoconferences are not appropriate for problem solving because the medium prevents them from reading nonverbal cues. But full-motion conference set-ups, in which the entire conference room and all the participants are visible at each location, do not interfere with a person's ability to see facial expressions and "read" shifts in attitude. Depending on the size of the screen, the camera's ability to focus in on a participant may even enhance some nonverbal cues. Freeze-frame set-ups, however, do not work well for problem-solving meetings because participants see only the head of the person speaking on the television monitor—and that picture changes only at intervals.

One plus in using a full-motion videoconference for problem solving is that it allows you to relax one of the general rules about meetings—that all participants be at about the same hierarchical level in the organization. Even though peers may still find it easier to have an open exchange than people at different levels, something about communicating at a distance seems to make discussions between top management and middle managers easier and more productive. As one person put it, "If I say something that makes the vice-president mad, at least I've got a 3,000-mile head start."

Other generalizations about making problem-solving meetings work—that participants know each other, that they have about the same level of knowledge of the problem at hand, and that they be equally familiar with the problem-solving techniques used in the organization—are as important, if not more important, in videoconferences as they are in conventional meetings. Even with everything in its favor, though, a videoconference cannot promote successful problem solving in all instances. In fact, for major projects that involve assembling a task force of people who know each other but do not normally work together, it's usually worthwhile to hold the initial meeting with everyone in one room to work out the preliminaries and divvy up the tasks, and to use videoconferences during the middle stages of the project to keep the participants focused on the goal. At the end, it's a good idea to bring everyone back together for the final report and debriefing.

Another kind of problem-solving meeting that isn't appropriate for videoconferencing is one that deals with highly sensitive issues—either very confidential matters or issues that would arouse intense emotions that shouldn't be handled "on stage"—either because they would embarrass people or because they would be unlikely to resolve themselves quickly. In general, any topic dealing with promotions, firings, or performance evaluations would fall in this category.

Screenings and interviews. Some companies have used or are trying out the use of videoconferences to screen applicants or consultants instead of footing the bill for an airline ticket. These uses, however, border on what we have categorized as "sensitive" and, at least at this stage, cannot be described as an unqualified success. It's anxiety-provoking enough to be in an interview without the added burden of having a camera put you on center stage. As a result, this form of interview may not provide an accurate reading of individual talents. On the other hand, should it become a commonplace procedure among large organizations, people will, as they always have, learn to adapt.

Formal presentations to a number of locations. One-way video, two-way audio systems are designed to permit people at one location to talk to and to be seen by people gathered in as many as a hundred locations. The presenter's picture and voice are transmitted and, while members of the audience can participate by making statements or asking questions, their pictures are not transmitted. Some firms have this equipment at their corporate headquarters with receiving locations at various divisions scattered around the country. These firms use their video conference systems mainly for employee meetings and training sessions.

This set-up works well when communicating with external audiences who do not need to participate in making a decision. Automobile companies have used it to introduce new models or to relay changes in parts prices, and drug companies have used it effectively to introduce new products. In this connection, it recently proved valuable to Johnson & Johnson, who used this set-up in

1982 when it had to regain public confidence in tamper-proof packaging of over-the-counter drugs.

Negotiations. Videoconferences are usually inappropriate for negotiations. Negotiations generally start in earnest only after positions have already hardened; breaking down the barriers to communication is extremely time-consuming—and in videoconferences, time is surely money. In the first place, the usual picture of the other participants is a frontal view, and people facing each other directly are least likely to be congenial. In the second place, it is psychologically easier to pull the plug on a videoconference than to storm out of a conference room.

Negotiations may depend on playing games, another reason videoconferences don't work. If more than two people are involved on each side, it is also impossible to "work the meeting"—for example, teaming up with someone, one of you playing the "bad guy" and the other playing the "good guy," so that together you get what you want. Such sophisticated meeting games require split-second timing and continual nonverbal feedback. There's little chance they'll work in a full-motion videoconference, and no hope at all in a fixed-frame videoconference.

Technical problem solving. Engineers and technical people, such as computer programmers and systems analysts, frequently call a meeting when something goes wrong—to establish the dimensions of the problem, make a stab at determining the cause, devise strategies for solving it, or allocate pieces of it to each person in an effort to find a solution. For such groups, the capability of transmitting visual data (engineering drawings, for example) to several locations simultaneously makes videoconferences tremendously productive. For meetings of this type, freeze-frame is more than adequate and black-and-white will generally suffice.

Will a Videoconference Be More Economical than a Face-to-Face Meeting?

The expectation, almost always, is that a videoconference will save a significant amount of money. Therefore, they are usually considered when the potential participants are separated by great distances or when travel arrangements are difficult to make. The true cost of any meeting involving travel, however, goes beyond simple monetary considerations. Maximizing the productivity of the participants frequently weighs in favor of a videoconference. After all, time wasted making airplane connections could be spent making executive decisions. And, while many work in the airplane, some find it difficult to do so. Others find that crossing time zones so disrupts their bodily rhythms they cannot work for hours, perhaps even a full day after a long trip.

The cost and inconvenience of long-distance travel is not always at issue, however; some companies use videoconferences simply to link offices scattered around a metropolitan area. They find it cuts down on the general wear and tear involved in travel, even when the distances are relatively short.

Are All the Key People Willing and Able to Participate?

Sometimes, circumstances make a videoconference seem like the only solution. A key participant may be unable to leave home base because of a pressing business or family problem, or there's a crisis that demands immediate response from several persons at different locations, or several participants have so many competing demands on their time that an electronic meeting is the only way of getting them together. In addition, some CEOs virtually demand videoconferences to save themselves travel time. However, there are managers who simply won't agree to a videoconference. One CEO we know, when approached to participate in a videoconference, snorted, "I don't need to see a person to get him to agree to a decision—I just pick up the phone and the problem is solved." If you work for someone like this, forget the videoconference, no matter how appealing the idea—a meeting without all the key decision makers is a wasted exercise.

Others, who have no concrete reasons for objecting to a videoconference, may be afraid of the technology or uneasy about "TV" being used for work instead of recreation. Trying something new also makes most people anxious about making fools of themselves in public—and filming makes their first efforts very public.

Objections to videoconferences may come from middle managers as well as executives. In addition to the usual fears, these managers may see travel as a "perk"—a reward for reaching a certain level in the organization. If participants view a videoconference as depriving them of a privilege they regard as one of the fruits of their labor, their suppressed resentment may express itself as unwillingness or failure to engage in discussion, and, at worst, as subconscious sabotage.

Not surprisingly, engineers and other technical people are the least likely to object to videoconferencing on anything other than objective grounds—their participation can usually be taken for granted.

Some organizations may be more open to experimenting with videoconferences than others. If there's a "flipchart culture," and people are accustomed to a great deal of structure and a rigidly controlled presentation format, they'll be too busy focusing on the visuals as they come along every two minutes to worry about the loss of the human element. If, however, people in the organization who are used to rolling up their sleeves and thrashing out problems side by side, they may be put off by the formality of the videoconference. Unless properly introduced to the technology, people in these organizations will complain about imaginary problems with the equipment and use these complaints as an excuse never to use video facilities.

Preparing for a Videoconference

You need to prepare for any presentation and preparing for your first videoconference requires additional effort. Your first experience can influence all your subsequent encounters, so you'll want the experience to be positive. Whether you're to be a participant or a leader, you'll need to understand how the system works; how to signal the leader, if you are a participant, and how to manipulate the equipment and signal the participants, if you are a leader. Besides understanding the mechanics, it is important for you to

- Dress for the camera's eye
- Establish a relationship with the other participants before the conference
- Create special visuals

Dress for the Camera's Eye

More and more videoconference studios are depending on natural light and, as a result, some of the old rules about dressing for the camera no longer apply. However, the medium still imposes some limitations on what you can wear. Obviously, you'll leave the zebra-striped dress or the garish plaid tie in your closet (you wouldn't wear either one to an on-site presentation), but any strong pattern is out—its lines will be translated by the camera into a wavy movement—the garment may actually appear to be jerking slightly. Wearing white is a less obvious pitfall. Too much white tends to make your facial tones very dark, or the white will bleed into a light-colored background. Red also bleeds into some backgrounds. Neutral tones, as in a beige or grey suit with a neutral colored shirt or blouse, are preferable.

If you are participating in a freeze-frame videoconference, only your face may be visible to the other participants. If you're a woman, wearing fussy blouses and large jewelry, including exaggerated earrings, chokers, and large brooches, will draw attention away from your face, and you'll diffuse the power of what you're saying.

Establish a Relationship with Other Participants

Relationships are easiest to establish and maintain if everyone can see everyone else, talk and listen face-to-face, and give each other immediate feedback. Most people need to spend time with each other before they can work together effectively. People unknown to each other tend to be stuffy and to communicate with extra formality at first. There's a definite need in the beginning of any working relationship to test the responses of others. Only after some time can most people let their defenses down sufficiently to work together with maximum effectiveness.

Getting to know other participants is especially important in a freeze-frame videoconference to compensate for the missing cues that give you insight into someone else's true attitude toward a proposal or another person. Since a picture is transmitted only every few minutes, the brief cocking of an eyebrow or a slight smile is easily lost. Similarly, gestures that are caught on camera may be awarded undue importance. For example, a quick shot of someone leaning back in her chair may not be sufficient to tell you whether she's expressing disinterest or suffering from muscle fatigue. Short of having continuous viewing of every participant, it is the degree to which you know someone that allows you to quickly judge the significance of gestures or expressions. If it's impossible to meet in person, try to call them on the phone and establish the relationship that way. If that, too, isn't feasible, whether you are leading or participating in the conference, pay special attention to the audience analysis questions in Chapter 2.

Create Special Visuals

In planning your visuals, ask the managers of the viedoconferencing studio and anyone else who has experience for advice. Since the capability of generating visuals is one of the reasons for going to the expense of holding a videoconference, making effective graphs and charts always pays off.

The design principles we cite in Chapter 5 generally apply to visuals for a videoconference as well. Because some distortions are inherent in the transmission process, it is especially important to concentrate on keeping text brief and graphics simple.

If your videoconference studio has a camera with a zoom lens, you can use a simple 3- × 5-inch card as easily as a large flipchart. In fact, the television camera is actually more successful at blowing up than reducing visuals. Cards can be prepared easily, either by typing (using a strong pica type as opposed to a fine-serif elite) or by neatly lettering with black felt-tipped marking pens. If the videoconference room is equipped with an overhead camera, you might find it desirable to create your visuals with felt-tip markers on 8½- × 11-inch tablets. The speaker can then simply place the visuals on the table and focus the camera on them. For flipcharts, letters should be at least 1½ inches high, but 2½ inches to 3 inches is better. The 3:4 screen ratio demands that flipchart visuals be designed to be horizontal rather than vertical, which is not the conventional flipchart shape. For overhead transparencies the proportion used should be 2:3 (close to the 7½ × 9½ inches usually prescribed)—otherwise part of the graph or chart will be lost when projected.

Although blueprints or engineering drawings are too large to transmit in their entirety, it's possible to cover parts of them and focus on the remaining segments. Photographs, particularly Polaroid prints, can be transmitted by most systems. Three-dimensional objects can be situated in front of a tripod camera and shot that way.

In general, use originals rather than copies of your visuals, especially when using pressure-sensitive lettering. In copies, the text may be too light to transmit well or the copying process may result in broken letters.

If you intend to develop visuals during the meeting, perhaps as a way of keeping track of decisions or new ideas, try to get into the studio ahead of time to experiment with different kinds of pens, letters, and colors. Although facsimile transmission may be available, using it during the conference creates the same problems as distributing handouts during a regular meeting.

Managing the Technology and the People as Conference Leader

Leading a full-motion videoconference is much like leading a face-to-face meeting. Leading a freeze-frame videoconference, however, is much harder than either. Not only does the technology distort your "feel" for the politics of the situation, it demands your attentive management throughout.

Handle the Mechanical Details

Although the technical part of the job continues to get simpler (one new system uses only one camera and one screen and is totally automatic—that is, no external operator is needed), as conference leader you should always arrive at the conference site early enough to check out the equipment and make sure that the cameras are able to pick up the visuals.

At commercial videoconference studios, personnel are available to help you with the equipment. Nevertheless, always make sure you try everything yourself—watching someone else do it isn't enough. This is true even if your console has only a few buttons for the various cameras. If no technicians will be on the scene during the videoconference (and they may be asked to leave if the conference deals with proprietary information), find out whom to call should something go wrong. Even if you're an inspired tinkerer, you shouldn't count on being able to get things running again on your own, and you cannot afford this kind of disruption.

Limit the Agenda

Thus far, experience indicates that people tire more easily in a videoconference than they do in a face-to-face meeting. Whether this is because of a lack of familiarity with the surroundings, the stress of focusing on a screen rather than a group of people, a fidgety concern about the cost per minute, or some combination of these factors, it appears that thirty minutes and three topics is about as much as people can effectively handle in this medium. In setting the objective and the agenda you must keep this in mind.

Brief Participants

Each participant should be notified of the videoconference well in advance, and notification should include time, date, and place of the videoconference. For a problem-solving session, participants should also be sent any data or background information they will need. In addition, depending on the circumstances and the degree of familiarity the participants have with the technology, they should be sent such advance materials as:

- a letter introducing the moderator (or leader) and a photograph
- biographies of the participants, with photographs
- the agenda
- a diagram of the room layout
- instructions for operating any equipment or pictures of the control console

If you're using an outside facility, include a map that shows how to get there.

As you can see, briefing documents are more extensive for videoconferences than for other kinds of meetings. But videoconferences are also more expensive, at least up front, and special care must be taken to use conference time efficiently.

Monitor the Process

As leader you must be certain someone is "in charge" at each site to introduce participants to each other and take care of details. Most face-to-face meetings are preceded by some informal talk and banter. The same social warm-up is perhaps even more important in this situation. The more closely your videoconference resembles a face-to-face meeting, the more relaxed participants will be. Arrange for informal talking time if at all possible.

If the conference includes a presentation of some kind, be sure the person making the presentation familiarizes himself or herself with the facilities, and that his or her visuals are appropriate to the medium.

Introductions, always important, are vital in a freeze-frame videoconference when the only person on view is the person who is speaking. At minimum, open the meeting by calling on each person and transmitting his or her picture to relieve participants of the feeling that they are talking into a void and to give everyone a face to go with the voice. At this time, you can say a few words about the participants or ask them to identify themselves. They should also introduce themselves each time they speak. Even though it seems somewhat contrived for Joan to say "This is Joan in St. Louis" before talking, it is immensely helpful to others in keeping the discussion from getting bogged down. Introduce everyone present in the studio, even those who are observers, and call on each by name rather than their location. If someone is called away during the meeting, mention the departure to avoid the embarrassing situation of having a participant address someone who is no longer there.

During the conference you must juggle the details of the discussion as well as the electronics. Given the expense of videoconferences, the techniques of summarizing, repeating, and staying on a time schedule (see Chapter 8) are even more important than in a face-to-face meeting. Make sure that new and complex ideas are given sufficient discussion time. Talking about anything complex is more difficult electronically than in a face-to-face meeting, even when you have sent advance materials. Participants may fight the technology in some way or be so eager to finish and get off camera that they'll pretend to understand when they do not. In this setting, asking for questions may not elicit them, so summarizing at regular intervals is very important.

Some videoconference consoles allow the moderator to hit a pause button and talk privately with others at his or her site. It is hard to imagine a situation in which using this method of excluding others would be advisable. Those left out are guaranteed to feel insulted.

The moderator is also responsible for soliciting feedback, both during the conference itself and afterward, possibly by distributing written forms. In the early stages of introducing videoconferences to an organization, obtaining feedback can make the difference between having people collaborate and having them resist the technology and spread their negative reaction through the organization.

Making an Effective Contribution as a Participant

If the videoconference will be held in-house, you will be able to try out the equipment in advance and become comfortable with the surroundings, the way your voice sounds over the microphone, and the way you look on the television monitor. Once you're familiar with the equipment, participating in a videoconference is less intimidating. It will probably take several encounters, however, before you will be comfortable enough with the form to truly concentrate on the substance of your contribution. Some tips to follow:

Try to keep a friendly expression, especially for a freeze-frame setup. Because your picture will be transmitted only intermittently, you don't want to be "caught" with a frown or in the midst of some nervous gesture. If you're speaking, use as much energy as you can muster—as some of it seems to get lost in the transmission. If you suddenly notice that you're on camera, don't stare fixedly into the lens. Instead try to look both at the camera and at others in your location. Viewers in other locations don't appreciate glassy-eyed stares. If you're in a full-motion videoconference in which the whole group is on camera at each site, remember that viewers do look at participants as well as at the speaker.

Always introduce yourself when you speak. If there are a great many participants and no one has bothered to send along your picture, the people at other locations will not necessarily remember who you are and may miss your comment trying to find out.

Don't engage in conversations with others at the site. This isn't good practice in any meeting, but in videoconferences with voice-activated microphones the side conversation will trigger the mike and ruin the audio transmission for the person legitimately speaking. For the same reason, try to keep casual sounds to a minimum—nervous coughing and clearing the throat will also activate your microphone.

Use good judgment when taking notes. If you're a doodler, be aware of the overhead camera and keep caricatures of other participants or pithy written comments out of camera range.

Listen carefully to what others are saying. This advice seems obvious until you consider that you cannot take advantage of the nonverbal cues you're accustomed to in normal meetings and you are likely to be distracted by the setting. Listen to the words and the meaning behind them. In the ideal setup, the camera and monitor are located close together so you have the feeling of talking to the other person rather than to the camera. In a less than ideal arrangement you will have to concentrate to overcome the distractions of the technology.

As the technology improves and its advantages become clear, videoconferences will be used more and more often. In addition to its cost-saving potential, this medium could change the way organizations function. As more people get access to information from far-flung locations, for example, executives will no longer have an information monopoly—traditionally one of the underpinnings of power. In addition, the control and reward systems of organizations may change. Once location no longer determines exposure, people of merit can be recognized no matter how far they are from corporate headquarters. Although the exact nature of these changes can't yet be foreseen, it is clear that the confidence- and competence-building techniques we have discussed in this book will be as valuable in a videoconference as they are in a conference room.

SUMMARY

To participate effectively in a videoconference, you'll need to know how the equipment works, and how to

- Decide whether a videoconference is appropriate by judging whether
  —the objective of the meeting fits the medium
  —most of the factors that lead to successful meetings are present
  —the cost is less than a face-to-face meeting in money, time, and human energy
  —the key people will participate
- Prepare for a videoconference by
  —dressing for the camera
  —establishing a relationship with the other participants
  —creating special visuals
- Manage the technology and the people as the conference leader
  —handle the mechanical details
  —brief the participants
  —monitor the process
- Make an effective contribution as a participant
  —keep a friendly open expression
  —introduce yourself
  —don't engage in side conversations
  —listen carefully

Afterword

In this book we have laid out a process for developing and delivering a management presentation, and we have considered how to apply our techniques to other situations. To become comfortable and competent in this arena will take practice, but it will pay off, especially as methods of communication change over the coming years, as we expect they will. The current wave of new technologies will not only increase communication demands, for example, but will alter power relationships: People will gain access to information previously denied them, and reward systems will shift as those who communicate most effectively in a range of media advance more rapidly than their less articulate counterparts.

For some people, neither conventional nor futuristic forms of presentations will ever be enjoyable, except as an opportunity to demonstrate competence. But we do believe that everyone can learn effective techniques for presenting ideas and programs successfully in any kind of setting—from a hallway conversation to a full-dress presentation in a videoconference. In addition, by sharing what you have learned with others, you will help them make more effective presentations as well.

CHECKLISTS, GUIDELINES, AND WORKSHEETS.

The checklists, guidelines, and worksheets in this Appendix appeared in the text. They are all designed to help you approach specific steps in the process of developing, giving, and evaluating a presentation. Reviewing them will refresh your memory and help you pay attention to the details that give polish to a presentation.

Guidelines for Selecting an Oral or Written Presentation

Select an oral presentation if you answer yes to these
questions:
- Is the topic controversial?
- Do the people involved need to ask questions to
  understand the material?
- Is immediate action necessary?
- Can participants get together easily?

Select a written presentation if you answer yes to these
questions:
- Does the audience need time to understand and absorb
  the material?
- Is a permanent record necessary to guard against
  misinterpretation?
- Is a discussion unimportant at this stage?

AUDIENCE PROFILE

My objective in making this presentation (underline action):

Who is the decision maker or decision makers?

How much does the decision maker know about the situation?

How does the decision maker view the situation?

How will the decision maker react to the proposal?

What is the decision maker's style?

Who else will attend the presentation?
What are their views of the proposal?

Who else will be affected by this presentation?

What's the next step?

What is my revised objective or fallback position?

WORKSHEET FOR DEVELOPING CRITERIA

Limits of Freedom

_____

_____

Negotiable Criteria	Weight	Reasons for Weight
_____	_____	_____
_____	_____	_____
_____	_____	_____
_____	_____	_____
_____	_____	_____
_____	_____	_____
_____	_____	_____
_____	_____	_____
_____	_____	_____

TRADE-OFF WORKSHEET

Criteria	Rank	Assigned Value	Score	Reason for Value Assigned

Alternative A:

× =

× =

× =

Total Score =

Alternative B:

× =

× =

× =

Total Score =

ORGANIZATION TREE WORKSHEET

Main Point
(What you want
the reader
to remember)

Major Support Points
(Must relate to
the main point
in the same way)

**Detailed
Support Points**

Checklist for Organization Tree

- Is the main point the one concept you want the audience to remember? (This statement will be the recommendation or the overriding generalization about the analysis.)

- **Do the major support points all relate to the main point in the same way?** (In a recommendation these will all be *reasons based on criteria*; in an evaluation of alternatives, either *alternatives* or *criteria*; in an implementation plan, *steps*; in a progress report, the *parts* of the analysis.)

- **Do the points to the right of any assertion all relate to that assertion in the same way?**

- **At each level of inference, does the statement generalize about the assertions to the right of it and about nothing else?**

WORKSHEET FOR DEVELOPING A BEGINNING

What is this presentation about? (This answer should be your recommendation or conclusion, the main point of your organization tree.)

Why is this presentation important to my audience? (This statement should describe what went wrong, what may go wrong, or what opportunity exists. It may help to ask yourself "What will happen if my proposal is not accepted?")

How will I develop the argument? (List your major support points, which constitute the body of your presentation.)

What must the audience know to understand the argument? (Check your organization tree with the audience profile in mind. Does the audience need any further information about the problem? Are there criteria that must be mentioned?)

Storyboard

Thesis Statement:

Supporting Statements:	**Data: Charts, Tables**

Transition Sentence:

Guidelines for Selecting a Visual Medium

Considerations	Flipcharts	Overheads	Slides
Audience size	Under 20 people	About 100 people	Several hundred people
Degree of formality	Informal	Informal or formal	Formal
Design complexity	Simple	Simple; can be made on office copier	Anything that can be photographed
Equipment and room requirements	Easel and chart	Projector and screen; shades to block light	Projector and screen; dim lighting
Production time	Drawing time only	Drawing or typing time; may be copied instantly	Design and photographing time plus at least 24 hours production time
Cost	Inexpensive unless professionally drawn	Inexpensive unless professionally designed or typeset	Relatively expensive

Guidelines for Designing Text Visuals

- Use no more than four to six lines of text.
- Limit each line to forty characters.
- Use phrases rather than sentences.
- Use upper and lowercase type.
- Use a simple typeface.
- Use bullets or Arabic numerals for listing.
- Allow the same amount of space at the top of each visual.
- Use color, boldface or large-sized type for emphasis.

Guidelines for Selecting Chart Forms

Graphic Form	Function
Line chart	Change in variables over time
Bar chart	Comparison of variables at one time or several points in time
Divided bar chart	Comparison of variables and their components at fixed times
Pie chart	Relationship of components to each other or to the whole
Diagram	Parts of a process, structure, or unit
Map	Relationship of geographical locations

Guidelines for Designing Graphic Visuals

- Limit data on a visual to what is absolutely necessary.
- Label axes, data lines, and chart areas when necessary for understanding.
- Keep chart lines thinner and lighter than data lines, omit grid lines, and don't smooth data lines.
- Use as few tick marks and numbers as possible and use rounded numbers.
- Make the spaces between bars narrower than the bars themselves.
- Don't exaggerate data points.
- Use color to highlight your message.
- Use headings to reinforce your point.

Guidelines for Making Overheads

- Work within a horizontal 7½ × 9½-inch space.
- Work on graph paper with light blue grids.
- Check overheads for readability of type size.
- Use the most professional lettering available.
- Use light lettering on a dark transparency if possible.
- Use transparencies of one color only.
- Use no more than one overlay on any overhead.
- Secure transparencies to cardboard frames.
- Number each transparency.

Guidelines for Using Overheads

- Be certain you are familiar with the operation of the projector.
- Turn the projector off whenever you are not discussing the points shown on a transparency.
- Be certain neither you nor the projector blocks anyone's view.
- Don't turn your back to the audience.
- Use a pencil rather than your finger to note a detail on the transparency.
- Write on a transparency only if you are very confident.

Guidelines for Making Flipcharts

- Choose a chart size that is appropriate for the design, your height, size of the audience.
- Draw your art to fit the vertical shape of the chart.
- Make lettering dark enough and large enough to be read by everyone in the audience.
- While you're preparing the charts, leave several blank pages between each one to allow for corrections or additions.
- Prior to your presentation, remove all but one blank page before each visual.

Guidelines for Using Flipcharts

- Securely attach the flipchart to the easel.
- Adjust the easel height before the presentation.
- Leave a blank page on top at the beginning of your presentation and turn to a blank page when there is no relevant visual.
- Grasp the visual in the middle to flip it.
- Always face your audience.

Guidelines for Designing Slides

- Design visuals for continuous viewing.
- Allow sufficient production time.
- Design all visuals based on the 2-to-3 ratio of a slide.
- Photograph boldface, simple, large-sized type.
- Follow the guidelines for making overheads.

Guidelines for Using Slides

- Check the position and order of the slides in your carousel or tray.
- Use your slides as notes.
- Rehearse with the projectionist.
- Use a conventional pointer.

Checklist
Presentation Logistics

Presentation Topic _____

        Date _____ Time _____

        Location _____ Contact Person _____

Presenter _____

Number of participants _____ Announcements sent (date) _____

Person responsible for setting up _____ Tel. No. _____

Seating arrangement (including number of chairs) _____

Location of restrooms _____

Location of telephones _____

Visual equipment _____

Lectern? _____ Microphone? _____ Lavalier? _____

Water/pitcher/glasses _____

Refreshments _____

    (Person responsible _____Tel. No. _____)

Handout materials _____

Checklist

Supplies

visuals
extra projector bulbs
spare parts for projector
converter plug
extension cord(s)
felt-tipped pens (different colors)
masking tape
stick pins
extra eyeglasses
chalk
erasers
blank transparencies
pointer
tent cards
extra handouts
extra agendas
marking pens for transparencies
lozenges

———————
———————

Checklist for Evaluating Yourself as Leader

- Was the agenda appropriate to the purpose?
- Was the meeting timely?
- Was consensus reached on a sufficient number of items?
- Did I prepare participants adequately?
- Was everyone who could provide vital information included?
- Did I encourage participation?
  —Did I cut anyone off too soon?
  —Did I keep people from rambling?
  —Did I call on everyone who wanted to speak?
- Did I let someone else control the meeting? If so, why?

Checklist for Evaluating Yourself as Participant

- Did I concentrate on the argument?
- Did I add anything new to the general understanding of the problem or did I "grandstand"?
- Were my contributions stated in positive rather than negative terms?
- Were my remarks complete but concise?

Guidelines for Ghostwriting

- Follow the rules for writing a speech.
- Consult frequently with the person giving the speech about
  —audience analysis
  —the main point
  —the organization
  —the tone
- Hold to the line of argument if irrelevant ideas are introduced.
- Don't substitute your ideas for those of the speechmaker.
- Make sure the person giving the speech knows who's responsible for arrangements.